CliffsNotes™

Investing in Mutual Fund

By Juliette Fairley

IN THIS BOOK

- Understand the different kinds of mutual funds

- Learn how experienced investors evaluate funds

- Make sense of mutual fund terms and jargon

- Pick a fund that matches your financial goals

- Reinforce what you learn with CliffsNotes Review

- Find more mutual fund information in CliffsNotes Resource Center and online at www.cliffsnotes.com

IDG Books Worldwide, Inc.
An International Data Group Company
Foster City, CA • Chicago, IL • Indianapolis, IN • New York, NY

IDG
BOOKS
WORLDWIDE

About the Author

Juliette Fairley is a personal finance writer whose work has appeared in *USA Today, The New York Times, Investor's Business Daily,* and other publications. Her first book, *Money Talks: Black Finance Experts Talk to You about Money,* was published in 1998 by John Wiley & Sons.

Publisher's Acknowledgments

Editorial

Senior Project Editor: Mary Goodwin

Acquisitions Editor: Mark Butler

Copy Editor: Linda S. Stark

Technical Editor: John C. Eisenbarth

Production

York Production Services

IDG Books Indianapolis Production Department

CliffsNotes Investing in Mutual Funds

Published by

IDG Books Worldwide, Inc.

An International Data Group Company

919 E. Hillsdale Blvd.

Suite 400

Foster City, CA 94404

www.idgbooks.com (IDG Books Worldwide Web site)

www.cliffsnotes.com (Cliffs Notes Web site)

Library of Congress Catalog Card No.: 99-64850

ISBN: 0-7645-8517-7

Printed in the United States of America

10 9 8 7 6 5 4 3 2 1

1O/SQ/QY/ZZ/IN

Distributed in the United States by IDG Books Worldwide, Inc.

Distributed by CDG Books Canada Inc. for Canada; by Transworld Publishers Limited in the United Kingdom; by IDG Norge Books for Norway; by IDG Sweden Books for Sweden; by IDG Books Australia Publishing Corporation Pty. Ltd. for Australia and New Zealand; by TransQuest Publishers Pte Ltd. for Singapore, Malaysia, Thailand, Indonesia, and Hong Kong; by Gotop Information Inc. for Taiwan; by ICG Muse, Inc. for Japan; by Norma Comunicaciones S.A. for Colombia; by Intersoft for South Africa; by Eyrolles for France; by International Thomson Publishing for Germany, Austria and Switzerland; by Distribuidora Cuspide for Argentina; by LR International for Brazil; by Ediciones ZETA S.C.R. Ltda. for Peru; by WS Computer Publishing Corporation, Inc., for the Philippines; by Contemporanea de Ediciones for Venezuela; by Express Computer Distributors for the Caribbean and West Indies; by Micronesia Media Distributor, Inc. for Micronesia; by Grupo Editorial Norma S.A. for Guatemala; by Chips Computadoras S.A. de C.V. for Mexico; by Editorial Norma de Panama S.A. for Panama; by American Bookshops for Finland. Authorized Sales Agent: Anthony Rudkin Associates for the Middle East and North Africa.

For general information on IDG Books Worldwide's books in the U.S., please call our Consumer Customer Service department at **800-762-2974**. For reseller information, including discounts and premium sales, please call our Reseller Customer Service department at **800-434-3422**.

For information on where to purchase IDG Books Worldwide's books outside the U.S., please contact our International Sales department at 317-596-5530 or fax **317-596-5692**.

For consumer information on foreign language translations, please contact our Customer Service department at **1-800-434-3422**, fax **317-596-5692**, or e-mail rights@idgbooks.com.

For information on licensing foreign or domestic rights, please phone **+1-650-655-3109**.

For sales inquiries and special prices for bulk quantities, please contact our Sales department at 650-655-3200 or write to the address above.

For information on using IDG Books Worldwide's books in the classroom or for ordering examination copies, please contact our Educational Sales department at **800-434-2086** or fax **317-596-5499**.

For press review copies, author interviews, or other publicity information, please contact our Public Relations department at **650-655-3000** or fax **650-655-3299**.

For authorization to photocopy items for corporate, personal, or educational use, please contact Copyright Clearance Center, 222 Rosewood Drive, Danvers, MA 01923, or fax **978-750-4470**.

Table of Contents

INTRODUCTION

You're looking at this book because you're interested in investing in mutual funds. That's good! You can see as you read the chapters that I'm a believer in mutual funds. For millions of people, they represent the safest, easiest, most affordable, and most profitable way to build an investment nest egg. Whether your financial objective is a secure retirement, a college education for your children, a new home, a business of your own, or some combination of these and other goals, mutual funds can help you reach your objectives.

In the past two decades, tens of millions of investors in the United States and abroad have discovered the advantages of mutual funds. As a result, the mutual fund industry enjoys the status of a booming business. Nearly 7,000 different mutual funds are now available, with almost $6 *trillion* in assets under management. (That's a 6 followed by 12 zeroes — wealth that's nearly unimaginable for most people.)

And this enormous pool of money is not being squandered on get-rich-quick schemes or some kind of paper-shuffling mumbo-jumbo designed to make a few Wall Street big shots wealthy. As you discover in this book, the money invested in mutual funds goes to buy stocks and bonds issued by businesses and government agencies around the world.

Knowledge about putting your money to work for you is especially important today. You and your family are beginning to take greater responsibility for your own financial well-being. In fact, you don't really have a choice. Here are some of the reasons:

■ The days of lifetime job security are gone. Today's businesses pride themselves on remaining "lean and mean," eliminating jobs whenever necessary to keep profits high.

You must take responsibility for your financial safety and not rely on a job that may evaporate tomorrow.

■ The days of the guaranteed company pension are gone. You may be self-employed, hold temporary positions, or change careers frequently, so you can't expect to retire from a company that has provisions to support you in old age. Even if you do stay at one firm for a long time, you may be expected to fund your own retirements.

■ Social Security has become a political football. You may not be able to count on Social Security to support you through retirement.

■ The cost of a college education or a home in a good neighborhood is higher than ever before. Without an aggressive program of saving and investing, you may not be able to afford the components of the "good life."

■ People are living longer than ever. That's good news, of course, but increased longevity also means that you need to plan for a retirement that lasts 20 to 40 years rather than 10 to 15.

This book, designed in the tradition of CliffsNotes, can help you get started investing in mutual funds, with simple, straightforward, basic advice in an easy-to-understand form. You won't learn *all* there is to know about mutual funds — that could take a lifetime. But you *will* learn all the facts you need to begin investing in mutual funds for profit — and even a little fun.

Why Do You Need This Book?

Can you answer yes to any of these questions?

■ Do you need to learn about mutual funds fast?

■ Don't have time to read 500 pages on mutual funds?

- Are you trying to save for a college education, a home, or a luxury car?

- Do you want to retire in comfort?

If so, then CliffsNotes *Investing in Mutual Funds* is for you!

How to Use This Book

This book is yours to use in whatever ways suit you best. You can either read the book from cover to cover or skip around from chapter to chapter. If you want quick and easy access to a particular topic, you can

- Use the index in the back of the book to find what you're looking for.

- Flip through the book looking for your topic in the running heads.

- Look for your topic in the Table of Contents in the front of the book

- Look at the In This Chapter list at the beginning of each chapter.

- Look for additional information in the Resource Center or test your knowledge in the Review section.

- Or, flip through the book until you find what you're looking for — I organized the book in a logical, task-oriented way.

Also, to locate important information quickly, you can look for icons strategically placed next to text. Here is a description of the icons you can expect to find throughout this book:

This icon introduces a fact, concept, or connection that's too important to forget.

This icon highlights a suggestion or idea that can save you time and energy, make you money, or make your life easier.

This icon introduces an important caution about a potentially dangerous situation or a mistake that's easy to make. If you ignore the information presented here, you're in jeopardy of losing time, money, or peace of mind. Don't worry — in each case, I also tell you what to do to avoid the danger.

Don't Miss Our Web Site

Keep up with the changing world of investing by visiting the CliffsNotes Web site at www.cliffsnotes.com. Here's what you find:

- Interactive tools that are fun and informative

- Links to interesting Web sites

- Additional resources to help you continue your learning

At www.cliffsnotes.com, you can even register for a new feature called CliffsNotes Daily, which offers you newsletters on a variety of topics, delivered right to your e-mail inbox each business day.

If you haven't yet discovered the Internet and are wondering how to get online, pick up *Getting on the Internet*, new from CliffsNotes. You'll learn just what you need to make your online connection quickly and easily. See you at www.cliffsnotes.com!

CHAPTER 1

BEFORE YOU INVEST IN MUTUAL FUNDS

IN THIS CHAPTER

- Analyzing your financial situation
- Setting financial goals
- Determining your appetite for risk
- Finding the money to begin investing
- Looking forward to feathering your nest over time

Before you invest in mutual funds — or any other investment — you need to ask yourself a few key questions. Most importantly, you must know where you are going before you start the journey. One key to investing wisely is knowing your financial goals. Are you investing for retirement, to finance a child's education, or to buy a home? Or are you investing for a short-term goal, like a new car or a great vacation? The answers to these questions greatly influence the kinds of investments that are right for your consideration — and financial outlay.

You also need to understand your own money personality — your willingness to take on risk and uncertainty when you invest, and how comfortable you are with markets that may change the value of your investments every day.

Finally, you need to figure out the source of your investment dollars: Where will you get the money to begin investing? Several avenues are worthy of exploring, even when budgets are tight: trimming needless expenses, reducing debt, and participating in an automatic investing plan at work. The sooner you start investing, the quicker the power of *compounding* — money growing over time — can work for you.

Setting Your Financial Goals

When you start thinking about investing in mutual funds, you need to first determine your financial goals. Why are you interested in investing? What do you hope to do with the profits you may make? Although mutual funds are well-known for their potential in retirement planning, investors use them to address a wide variety of financial goals.

You can think of financial goals as *short-term, long-term,* or a combination of the two.

Short-term goals

Short-term goals are those material targets you set your sights on hitting within one to three years from today. Typical short-term goals include

- A vacation next summer
- A new car to replace the old one you're driving now
- Upgraded appliances for your kitchen

All these goals have two things in common. First, they cost more money than most people expect in a single paycheck. Second, the amount of money needed to achieve any of these goals is manageable enough to enable most people with a steady income to accumulate the cash within one to three years — provided they save and invest.

When saving for a goal that is three years away or less, a practical investment option is a particular type of mutual fund called a *money market fund*. Money you invest in a money market fund grows slowly but steadily, with little fluctuation in value. You can read more about money market funds in Chapter 5.

Long-term goals

Long-term goals are those for which most people save and invest for longer than ten years. Most people have two main long-term goals:

■ A full-time college education for one or more children, including tuition and living expenses

■ A secure, comfortable, and enjoyable retirement

Long-term goals involve investing your money and leaving it in your investment until you need it, ten years or more in the future. Patience and persistence are key to long-term investments, in at least three ways:

■ You need to invest steadily, a few dollars every month, if you want your investment to grow.

■ You have to leave the money alone — don't withdraw cash every time you're tempted by a sale at the local mall or attracted by the sleek lines of a new model car.

■ You must accept the fact that most investments rise and fall in value. Resist the urge to panic when your investment takes a dip. The setback is probably only temporary.

The tendency of investments to rise and fall in value is called *volatility*. Maybe you've heard about stock-market crashes or other sudden drops in investment values; perhaps you've seen pictures of frightened investors screaming into their phones or even jumping out of windows in despair.

When volatility is extreme, anxiety is a normal reaction. The benefit of long-term investing is that market fluctuations don't matter as much. As a long-term investor, you have time for your investments to rebound — as they usually do.

Because a long-term investor has time to weather the ups and downs of a changing market, he or she can invest in relatively risky, volatile mutual funds. Read more about these types of funds in Chapter 4.

Although the stock market always rises and falls in the short term, the market's long-haul investment history shows that no other kind of investment grows so steadily or so much. Thus, long-term money generally belongs in the stock market, and stock funds are a great way to go.

Figure 1-1:   A place for you to list your short- and long-term goals.

Short-term goals	$$$	Time frame
☐ _____	_____	_____
☐ _____	_____	_____
☐ _____	_____	_____
☐ _____	_____	_____

Long-term goals	$$$	Time frame
☐ _____	_____	_____
☐ _____	_____	_____
☐ _____	_____	_____
☐ _____	_____	_____

A combination of goals

What if, like most people, you have both short-term and long-term goals? You probably want to save for retirement *and* for a new car. How do these dual goals affect your investment strategy?

The answer is simple: Divide the money you have to invest into two or more streams, and invest in more than one kind of mutual fund. Each month, set aside a certain amount of money for short-term goals, and invest those dollars in a fund that is low-risk, not very volatile, and safe — even though the growth of your money may not be spectacular.

At the same time, set aside another sum for long-term saving, and invest that money in more risky, more volatile stock funds, whose upside potential — that is, opportunity for truly impressive growth — is greater. This set of investments may rise or fall, month by month, but over time these funds are likely to outperform your short-term money — if you're patient enough to let it happen.

How much of your investment money should go toward short-term investing, and how much toward long-term? That depends on several factors, especially the relative importance of various financial goals to you and your age (which affects the length of time until you retire or send children to college). For many people, a 50/50 split is a reasonable starting point, to be adjusted as you see fit over time.

Dividing your investment money into two or more kinds of investments with different characteristics is known as *diversification.* Think of the basic law of diversification as "Don't put all your eggs in one basket." You reduce risk when you divide your money among different investments; even if one investment goes down in value, the other is likely to go up, balancing loss with profit and helping you come out ahead in the end.

I deal with diversification in Chapter 3. As you'll discover, avoiding having all your money tied up in any single investment is one of the basic principles of smart investing — and one of the main advantages you derive from any mutual fund investment.

Understanding Your Money Personality

In addition to determining your financial goals, you need to assess your personal relationship to money — specifically, your *risk tolerance.*

Some people are comfortable with the idea of investing their money in relatively risky or volatile investments. They have the patience — and the psychological stamina — to stay calm as the value of their investments rises and falls, confident that they'll win out in the end.

Others can't stand this kind of uncertainty. They want to know exactly what their investments will be worth one year, two years, and ten years from now, and they don't want to be bothered with tracking the ups and downs of the market. Where you fall on this spectrum is your risk tolerance, your ability to live comfortably with a degree of financial uncertainty.

Which kind of investor are you? Can you imagine yourself sleeping soundly at night while knowing that your investments may be changing in value on a daily or hourly basis? Are you excited by the idea of investing as a kind of game, with winners and losers, or does the thought of losing some of your hard-earned investment money make you feel a little queasy? The answers to these questions are vital clues to the right investment choices for you.

Tip

If you're not sure about your own risk tolerance level — as is true of many new investors — try this approach. Divide your investment money into two batches. Put one batch, perhaps three quarters of your money, into safe, secure investments. Put the rest into more risky, growth-oriented funds. (If you're starting from scratch, expect to take a little time to accumulate enough money to divide into two batches.) Then watch how these investments perform over the next two to three years.

Depending on how well you do with your "risk money," you may decide to gradually increase that investment, shift it to other types of funds, or reduce it. As you monitor your investments and make these kinds of decisions, your sense of your money personality becomes clearer. You learn exactly what degree of risk you're comfortable with, and you develop an instinct for putting together an investment plan that's both profitable and psychologically acceptable to you.

Finding the Money to Invest

Finding money to invest in mutual funds requires the discipline of *not* spending and sticking to a budget. You need a bit of willpower and real determination to make it happen. If you decide to take $100 to $500 a month out of your salary to invest, you can find ways to trim the fat.

Here are some ways to reduce your spending without suffering undue hardship:

- Cutting back on going out to eat
- Avoiding daily trips for pricey coffees, sodas, and snacks
- Quitting smoking
- Renting movies to watch at home instead of going to the local theatre
- Keeping your aging-but-still-running car a year or two longer

Paying yourself first

Make saving and investing a priority. One way to do this without feeling financially deprived is to "pay yourself first." That is, when you get your weekly or biweekly paycheck, *before* paying your usual bills — rent or mortgage, utilities, credit cards — set aside a regular amount for investing.

Put the predetermined sum — whether it's $100, $500, or even more — in a special savings account or write a check directly to the mutual fund of your choice. By allocating this money first, before you start spending on other things, you can more easily resist the temptation to skip a week or a month here and there along the investing trail. Furthermore, you may find that you hardly miss the extra money; you'll quickly adjust your spending habits to live on a little less each month, reinforced by the pleasure of watching your investment account grow.

Many employers offer special saving and investing programs, such as 401(k) plans, which can make paying yourself first even easier. Such programs provide for automatic deductions from your paycheck, with the money allocated to the investments of your choice, including mutual funds.

You may realize tax benefits from participating in such plans, and some employers even contribute extra money, matching the contributions you make. Ask where you work. If your company offers such a plan, start participating as soon as you can.

Trimming your credit card debt

The best way to improve your personal financial situation and to free up money for investing is by reducing your debt — especially costly credit card debt. In these days of easy credit, most people find their mailboxes stuffed daily with credit card offers from banks and other companies. It's temptingly easy to accept the offers, run up a balance with purchases, and then switch to yet another card.

The unwary person who owns and uses several credit cards can find himself carrying a total debt equal to half or more of his yearly income — an uncomfortable, costly, and dangerous way of life.

If you take the following steps to reduce the debt drain on your finances, you'll soon see your investment fund growing:

■ Pay off credit card balances as soon as you can. At interest rates of 17%, 18%, or even higher, these are among the most expensive loans offered anywhere. The longer you take to repay them, the more each purchase costs.

■ Start paying your total credit card balance each month rather than the minimum amount. This will force you to begin living on your current income instead of mortgaging your future for present purchases.

■ If you own a home, consider consolidating and paying off your credit card balances with a home equity loan. The interest rates on home equity loans are usually lower, and the interest may be tax deductible.

Putting Time to Work for You

Try to start investing regularly as soon as you can. Invested money grows by *compounding* — that is, the profits you earn on the money you invest generate additional profits, and these in turn generate more profits, for as long as you let your investment grow.

Compounding is a remarkably powerful wealth-building process that can turn relatively modest amounts of money into a fortune — provided you give the investment time to work.

Table 1-1 illustrates how compounding can work for you. The table assumes that you set aside $100 at the start of each month for investing purposes. Go down the table to the year that shows how long you expect to let your investment money grow. Then read across the table to see how much money you can expect to accumulate at various rates of return.

Table 1-1:   How Compounding Works for You

Growth of a $100/month investment at various rates of return, with compounding.

	Rate of Return				
Year	**4%**	**6%**	**8%**	**10%**	**12%**
1	$1,230	$1,240	$1,250	$1,270	$1,280
2	2,500	2,560	2,610	2,670	2,720

Continued

Table 1-1: How Compounding Works for You (continued)

Growth of a $100/month investment at various rates of return, with compounding.

	Rate of Return				
Year	4%	6%	8%	10%	12%
3	3,830	3,950	4,080	4,210	4,350
4	5,210	5,440	5,670	5,920	6,180
5	6,650	7,010	7,400	7,810	8,250
10	14,770	16,470	18,420	20,660	23,230
15	24,690	29,230	34,830	41,790	50,460
20	36,800	46,440	59,290	76,570	99,910
25	51,580	69,650	95,740	133,790	189,760
30	69,640	100,950	150,030	227,930	352,990
20	36,800	46,440	59,290	76,570	99,910
25	51,580	69,650	95,740	133,790	189,760
30	69,640	100,950	150,030	227,930	352,990

If you set aside $100 a month, after 12 months you save $100 × 12 = $1,200. However, as the table shows, if this invested money earned a 10% rate of return, it would be worth $1,270 at the end of the first year. With compounding, the investment would grow faster the second year, reaching a value of $2,670 — fully $270 more than the amount you actually invested. And by the end of the tenth year, the same account would have grown to $20,660, which is $8,660 more than the amount you actually invested.

When the time frame extends far into the future — 25 to 30 years, or even longer — the power of compounding becomes truly awesome. As you can see, the same $100 per month investment has the potential to grow, after 30 years, to over $227,000. If you manage to save two or three times more per month, your accumulated total would be two or three times greater.

CHAPTER 2

LEARNING ABOUT MUTUAL FUNDS

IN THIS CHAPTER

- Defining mutual funds
- Making money from owning a mutual fund
- Comparing closed-end and open-end funds

Mutual funds are a very popular means of investing money. A mutual fund pools money received from individual investors like you — often in modest amounts — to create a large investment fund. A professional fund manager with detailed knowledge of investing then puts this money to work for you. As the money grows over time, so does the value of your investment.

The money in mutual funds is usually invested either in stocks or in bonds. *Stocks* represent shares in the ownership of companies. When you own stocks, you share in the profits the companies enjoy, and when the value of the companies grows, so does the value of your stocks.

Bonds, on the other hand, represent money that has been borrowed by a company or a government agency. When the loan is repaid, the owner of the bond gets the money back with interest. When you invest in a *mutual fund,* your money goes with the money of many other people to buy stocks or bonds. As the mutual fund that owns the stocks or bonds profits from these investments, so do you.

What Is a Mutual Fund?

A mutual fund is an investment vehicle that pools the money of many investors to buy a large number of investments. By pooling small amounts of money invested by thousands of individuals, a mutual fund can invest in dozens of different stocks, bonds, and other securities. When you buy shares in the fund, you become a part owner of all those investments, and as those investments grow, so will your money.

When you buy a share in a mutual fund, you are participating in the performance of all the investments selected by the manager of the fund. Most individuals don't have the resources to invest in a wide range of stocks, bonds, or other investment vehicles, nor do they have the money to hire a professional money manager to choose investments for them (see Figure 2-1).

Figure 2-1: Mutual fund investments can cover a broad range of possibilities.

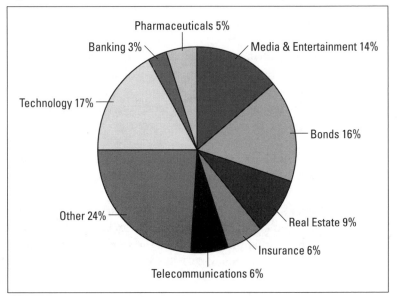

In order to understand how mutual funds work, you need to understand the difference between mutual funds and the stocks and bonds that are owned by a mutual fund.

A share of stock represents part ownership of a company. When you own a share of IBM, Walt Disney, General Motors, or Amazon.com, you own a (tiny) portion of that company. If the company's sales and profits increase, you benefit: You're likely to receive *dividends,* which are payments of a portion of a company's profits to shareholders. Plus, the value of your stock probably increases as the company prospers.

By contrast, a bond is like an IOU. A bond represents a loan of money to the managers of a business or a government agency; they promise to pay you back, with interest, over a specified period of time. You can buy and sell bonds on the open market (usually with the help of a financial professional called a broker). When you buy a bond, you are purchasing the promise of repayment with interest. Like shares of stock, bonds may rise and fall in value.

Bonds usually change in value based on changes in interest rates: In general, when interest rates rise, bonds fall in value, and vice versa (see Figure 2-2).

A mutual fund is a collection (or *portfolio*) of individual stocks, bonds, and (rarely) other kinds of securities that are generally of interest only to financial specialists. The mutual fund manager selects the stocks and bonds based on the investment objectives and style of the particular fund and on the manager's judgment as to which investments are likely to be most profitable. (In later chapters, I explain how you can determine the objectives and style of a particular fund and whether that fund is a good choice for you.) In general, if the manager selects wisely, investors in the mutual fund benefit; if the manager's choices are poor, the investors suffer.

Figure 2-2: As interest rates rise, bond values fall.

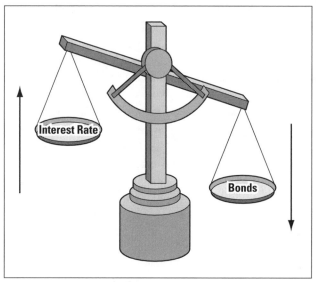

Thus, the main difference between a mutual fund and individual stocks and bonds is that the person who invests in a mutual fund owns shares in an entire portfolio of stock or bond investments, managed by a knowledgeable financial professional. It's like handing your investment money to an expert and saying, "Here — you pick some good investments for me, and send me the profits."

The sale and trading of mutual funds, stocks, and bonds is regulated by the Securities and Exchange Commission (SEC), a government agency that protects investors from fraud and theft. However, the value of your investment in a mutual fund (or an individual stock or bond) is not guaranteed by the SEC or by any other government institution.

You can lose money on a mutual fund investment — in an extreme case, even *all* your money. However, the safety track record of most mutual funds is quite good. In fact, since the passage of the Investment Company Act of 1940, which regulates mutual funds, no fund has collapsed or gone bankrupt.

How You Profit from a Mutual Fund

When you own shares in a mutual fund, you stand to profit in three different ways:

- Through any increase in the value of the stocks and/or bonds owned by the fund (the net asset value)

- Through any dividends paid to the fund by the companies issuing the stocks and/or bonds

- Through any profits earned by the fund when they buy and sell stocks or bonds (capital gains)

Net asset value

The value of the stocks and/or bonds owned by a mutual fund is usually stated in terms of net asset value (NAV). The number of securities in a fund may range from as few as 30 to as many as 120. As the value of the securities moves up and down, the NAV (and the purchase price) of your fund changes accordingly.

Net asset value is expressed as the value of all the securities (stocks and/or bonds) in the mutual fund portfolio divided by the number of shares of the mutual fund owned by investors. The resulting net asset value per share is the price at which shares in the fund can be bought or sold.

For example, if a mutual fund owned stocks with a total value of $1 billion dollars and investors owned 100 million shares of the fund, the net asset value per share would be $1 billion ÷ 100 million = $10. Thus, it would cost an investor $10 to buy a single share in the fund, and an investor who sold a share in the fund would receive $10 for it.

Because the values of stocks and bonds change from day to day, the NAV of any mutual fund also fluctuates on a daily basis. As the NAV of a fund you own rises, so does the value of your shares. When you decide to sell those shares, you receive more money than you paid for them, reflecting the higher value. (Of course, the NAV of a fund may sometimes fall.)

If you're interested, you can find the current NAV of many mutual funds listed in the business pages of your daily newspaper. Figure 2-3 contains a sample mutual fund listing, from *The New York Times* for July 13, 1999. Notice how the paper provides the following kinds of information:

- **Fund Family:** This is the company that owns and manages the specific mutual funds. Some companies, like Fidelity (shown in Figure 2-3), operate dozens of funds with various investment objectives and styles.

- **Fund Name:** Shown in abbreviated form, this is the name of the specific mutual fund. In this listing, "AggGrow" stands for Aggressive Growth, whereas "Bal" (a few lines down) translates to Balanced, and "Canada" names a fund that specializes in stocks of companies based in that country.

- **NAV:** The net asset value per share, as described earlier in this section, as of the end of the previous business day. In this sample listing, Fidelity's Aggressive Growth fund had a NAV of $43.57 per share.

- **Daily % Return:** Yesterday's change in value of NAV from the previous day. In the listing shown, the NAV of Fidelity's Aggressive Growth fund had fallen by 0.3% from the previous day. If you're an investor in the fund, you don't want to see a downward trend continue indefinitely.

- **Year to Date % Return:** This is the change in value of NAV from the start of the calendar year (actually, from

December 31 of last year). So far this year, Fidelity's Aggressive Growth fund has, in fact, grown aggressively — 40.2% in just a little over six months. (By contrast, the Canada fund, for example, has grown about 9.4% — still respectable for one-half of a year. You can learn much more about how to judge investment performance later in this book, especially in Chapter 7.)

Of course, the amount of money you make by investing in a fund won't match the Year-to-Date % Return shown in the newspaper, unless you happened to buy your shares precisely on December 31. But the Year-to-Date % Return is a useful gauge to how the fund is performing right now.

Figure 2-3: Typical listing of mutual fund data in a daily newspaper.

Fidelity				Fifth Third A				Growth A m	30.66	− 0.5	+ 5.9
AggGrow d	43.57	− 0.3	+40.2	Bal m	16.47	− 0.4	+ 5.2	Growth H m	29.17	− 0.5	+ 5.4
AstMgr	18.29	− 0.2	+ 6.9	Bdlnc m	11.83	+ 0.1	− 0.6	Growth Z	31.07	− 0.5	+ 6.0
AstMgrGr	20.18	...	+ 8.0	Cardinal m	20.19	− 0.2	+14.3	TaxFMN E f	10.14	+ 0.1	− 0.9
AstMgrln	12.42	+ 0.1	+ 3.3	Pinnacle f	38.38	− 0.2	+ 7.9	TaxFNatE f	10.73	+ 0.1	− 1.5
Bal	17.98	− 0.3	+11.2	QualGrow m	23.99	− 0.6	+12.0	USGovt A m	9.09	+ 0.1	− 1.6
BlChGrow	55.61	− 0.3	+10.4	**Fifth Third Inst**				USGovt E f	9.09	+ 0.1	− 1.4
Canada m	15.30	− 0.8	+ 9.4	Bal	16.48	− 0.4	+ 5.4	Value A m	14.23	− 0.8	+10.6
CapApr	26.29	− 0.3	+19.1	Eqlnc	15.67	− 0.3	+ 3.6	**Forum**			
CapInc d	10.11	...	+14.7	IntlEq	12.73	− 0.5	+ 5.3	InvBond f	10.07	...	− 1.7
CongrSt	414.02	− 0.3	+11.0	MidCap	16.24	− 0.9	+ 4.2	InvEquity f	13.79	− 0.5	+ 9.5
Contra f	64.01	− 0.3	+13.7	MuniBd	11.82	+ 0.1	− 1.6	InvHiGrBd f	9.71	+ 0.2	− 1.6
Contrall f	12.78	− 0.5	+14.7	OHTaxF	10.05	...	− 1.6	MEMuBond f	10.84	+ 0.1	− 0.3
ConvSec	21.13	− 0.1	+16.3	Pinacle	38.45	− 0.2	+ 8.0	TaxSvrBd f	10.35	...	− 0.7
Destin I m	29.06	− 0.4	+ 7.8	QualBd	9.66	+ 0.1	− 2.0	**Forward**			
Destinll m	15.98	− 0.4	+12.1	QualGr	24.05	− 0.6	+12.1	Equity	13.63	− 0.3	+12.8
DiscEq d	33.19	− 0.1	+13.2	USGovt	9.73	+ 0.1	− 0.3	GlobAstAl	10.67	− 0.1	+ 8.5
DivGrow	32.39	− 0.1	+12.7	**59 Wall Street**				GlobBond	9.81	+ 0.3	...
Divrlntl	19.69	− 0.5	+11.1	EuroEq	37.29	− 1.6	+ 1.6	SmCap	12.60	− 0.1	+10.6
EmgMkt m	9.91	− 0.9	+40.6	IntlEq	12.44	− 0.8	+13.6	**Founders**			
Eqlnc	62.16	− 0.5	+14.2	PacBEq	35.12	+ 0.5	+56.6	Bal b	12.26	+ 0.2	+ 1.8
Eqlnc II	32.42	− 0.5	+ 9.3	TaxEffEq b	12.92	− 0.5	+13.4	Discover b	32.06	− 0.4	+31.6
EuCapApr m	17.92	− 1.0	+ 0.3	TxFShint	10.32	...	+ 0.3	Frontier b	29.87	− 0.2	+17.1
Europe m	32.53	− 1.1	− 2.8	**First American A**				Grlnc b	7.66	− 0.3	+ 4.6
Exchange	272.62	+ 0.1	+10.2	AdjRtMgt m	8.09	...	+ 2.5	Growth b	23.03	− 0.3	+12.8
ExpMulNat m	22.83	− 0.3	+14.8	Bal m	14.29	− 0.3	+ 7.0	MidCap b	8.35	− 0.4	+12.2
Fidelity	40.82	− 0.4	+11.7	Eqlndex m	27.75	− 0.4	+13.9	Passport b	16.59	− 0.3	+11.1
Fifty f	21.54	...	+27.8	Fixln m	10.84	+ 0.1	− 2.0	WorldGro b	23.49	− 0.8	+ 6.5
Freelnc	11.25	...	+ 3.4	Intl m	15.01	− 0.1	+ 8.8	**Franklin Adv**			
GNMA	10.60	+ 0.2	+ 0.3	IntrmTm m	9.89	+ 0.1	− 0.8	AGEHiln	2.68	...	+ 2.8
GlobBal	18.08	− 0.2	+ 6.9	LgCapGr m	20.58	− 0.3	+17.0	GrowthAdv	35.07	+ 0.1	+11.5
Govtlnc	9.67	...	− 1.9	LgCapVal m	25.50	− 0.6	+15.1	USGovt	6.66	...	...
GrowCo	62.39	...	+23.3	MNTaxE m	10.97	...	− 0.7	**Franklin Group A**			
Growlnc	49.22	− 0.3	+ 7.8	MidCapGr m	13.32	− 0.7	+ 8.2	AGEHiln m	2.68	+ 0.4	+ 2.7
Hilnc d	12.62	+ 0.2	+ 9.8	RegEq m	20.15	− 0.3	+ 7.5	ALTaxFln m	11.40	+ 0.1	...
HongKChi m	14.24	− 1.5	+40.9	SmCpGrowA m	16.95	...	+11.4	ARMuBond m	10.66	...	− 0.9
InstShln	9.23	+ 0.1	+ 0.7	StrInc gn	9.28	+ 0.1	+ 0.4	AZInsTxF m	10.52	+ 0.1	− 0.9
IntBond	9.99	+ 0.1	+ 0.2	TaxE m	10.89	...	− 1.2	AZTaxFln m	11.05	+ 0.1	− 0.2
IntGovt	9.53	...	− 0.2	**First American B**				AdjUSGov m	9.32	...	+ 2.6
IntlBond	8.42	+ 0.4	− 5.0	Bal m	14.22	− 0.3	+ 6.6	AssetAlc m	10.79	− 0.2	+ 9.5
IntlGrInc	23.03	− 0.6	+10.1	Eqlndex m	27.55	− 0.4	+13.4	BalSheet m	33.30	− 0.1	+ 5.9
IntlVal	15.16	− 0.6	+12.5	LgCapVal m	25.22	− 0.6	+14.7	BioDisc m	27.45	+ 2.0	+ 8.6
InvGrlnll	10.77	− 0.6	+ 7.9								

Copyright © 1999 by *The New York Times*. Reprinted by permission.

The newspaper listings also include footnotes of various kinds, indicated by lowercase letters next to the fund names. Visually scan the newspaper page for an explanation of these cryptic letters. By looking up the explanations, you can learn, for example, that the small "d" next to "AggGrow" means that you can expect a "deferred sales charge" on Fidelity's Aggressive Growth fund. This is a worthwhile piece of information if you're considering buying shares in this fund. (I explain this and other mutual fund fees in Chapter 6.)

Dividends

Dividends are a portion of the profits earned by a company, which the company may distribute to their stockholders.

Not all companies pay dividends. Young, quick-growing companies may choose to reinvest all their profits in further company growth, spending the money to hire new employees, buy new machinery, or develop new business ideas. However, older, more-established companies often pay regular dividends — usually four times a year — to their shareholders, calculated on the basis of so many cents per share owned. For example, if a company decides to pay its shareholders a dividend of 50 cents per share, an individual who owns 200 shares of that company's stock will receive a check for $100.

When a mutual fund owns stock, the fund receives the dividends and distributes them to investors, usually in the form of additional fund shares. Thus, the value of your mutual fund investment grows when the stocks owned by the fund pay dividends.

Capital gains

The mutual fund manager buys and sells stocks and bonds continually, in response both to changing market conditions and to the flow of money into or out of the fund. When the manager sells a stock or bond at a higher price than he paid for it, the difference is a kind of profit known as a capital gain. As with dividends, the capital gains received by a mutual fund are distributed to owners of the fund, usually in the form of additional fund shares.

When tax time arrives, the Internal Revenue Service calls for varying treatments for the different kinds of profit you make when you own a mutual fund. Read Chapter 9 for a detailed explanation of how to pay the right amount of taxes — and no more — on the growth of your mutual fund investments.

Closed-End Funds versus Open-End Funds

The most popular kind of mutual fund is known as an *open-end fund.* (In fact, unless it's otherwise stated, you can assume that any mutual fund you hear or read about is an open-end fund.) An open-end fund continuously issues new shares and redeems old shares on demand.

When such a fund is popular, money flows in to the fund manager from investors who are eager to own shares. The manager then invests this new money in additional stocks and/or bonds. New shares in the fund are constantly being created.

By contrast, *closed-end funds* issue a fixed number of shares. After investors buy these shares, no more money can enter the fund. If you want to sell shares that you own, you don't sell them to the fund management firm, as with an open-end fund. Instead, the shares trade on an exchange, much like the trading of shares in the stock of individual companies. Thus, the price of a share in a closed-end fund is set by supply and demand: If investors are eager to buy the shares, the price rises; if not, the price falls.

Like an open-end fund, a closed-end fund has a net asset value, computed by dividing the total value of the fund's portfolio holdings by the number of shares. However, the shares of an open-end fund may sell at a *premium* to the NAV (that is, for more than the NAV) or at a *discount* to the NAV (that is, for less than the NAV).

For instance, if a particular closed-end fund has an NAV of, say, $15 per share, the actual price at which the shares trade may be higher (say, $18 per share) or lower (say, $11 per share).

Of course, you're better off buying shares of a closed-end fund at a discount rather than at a premium. In fact, experts generally advise investors to buy closed-end fund shares *only* when they're available at an attractive discount.

A mutual fund company may decide to offer a closed-end fund rather than an open-end fund for several reasons. The main consideration: a desire to *avoid* having too much money to invest.

With a closed-end fund, the fund manager knows how much money he must handle; he doesn't continually get new money to invest, as may be the case with an open-end fund. In some investment markets, closed-end may be a better way of doing business.

For example, an emerging market (that is, a new or relatively undeveloped business region, such as South America or Eastern Europe) may have only a limited number of good companies in which to invest. The manager of a fund specializing in such a market may worry about taking in more money than he can invest wisely. A closed-end fund solves this problem.

Tip

For the average investor, open-end funds are a better choice than closed-end funds. Newspapers and financial magazines cover open-end funds more extensively, which makes it easier to track them. They are more liquid than close-end funds — that is, easier and more convenient to buy and sell. And their prices are less volatile; upward and downward movement is slower and more predictable.

Some sophisticated investors are especially interested in closed-end funds, but they are probably not the best starting point for the individual who is new to mutual funds.

CHAPTER 3

RECOGNIZING THE PROS AND CONS OF MUTUAL FUNDS

IN THIS CHAPTER

- The advantages of investing in mutual funds
- Understanding diversification, liquidity, and shareholder services
- The disadvantages of investing in mutual funds
- Looking at the risks

No investment is right for everyone. Like any other investment, mutual funds have both advantages and disadvantages. The disadvantages are real, and you really need to understand the potential drawbacks before you invest. Nonetheless, for millions of people, mutual funds are the most convenient, safe, and profitable way to invest.

Advantages of Investing in Mutual Funds

Mutual funds invest in the same kinds of stocks and bonds that individual investors can (and do) buy — so why employ a middleman (the fund manager)? What benefits do you enjoy from investing through a mutual fund rather than purchasing directly?

Putting your money to work in mutual funds provides distinct advantages over other forms of investments. If, after you weigh the pros and cons, you decide to take the plunge, you're likely to come up with your own additions to the list of benefits.

Diversification

Diversification involves spreading your money around among several different kinds of investments in order to reduce the risk of concentrating in a single security (see Figure 3-1). When your investments are diversified, you don't take a major hit if any one investment performs poorly. Thus, the savvy investor avoids concentrating all her investments in the stock of a single company, or even a single industry.

Figure 3-1: Reducing your risk by diversifying.

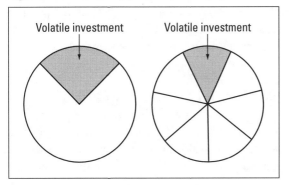

You may be lucky enough to work for a company that helps you invest through a 401(k) retirement plan or by awarding you *stock options* — the opportunity to buy the company's stock at a special, often discounted, price. Either way, you enjoy a great reward for being an employee.

But be careful — employees sometimes end up investing almost their entire savings in the stock of the company they work for. All is well as long as the company is flourishing. But if the industry suffers a downturn, or if your own company happens to go bankrupt, you may find that your investment is suddenly worth little or nothing.

Mutual funds also allow you to diversify your investments at a relatively low cost. Because of transaction costs (the fees charged when you buy or sell stock), you can waste time and money buying one or two shares of stock in a dozen different companies, which may be all that an investor with a couple of thousand dollars can afford. But the same investor can easily afford to invest in one or more mutual funds. Buying mutual fund shares makes you a part owner of many different types of stocks (or bonds), giving you the benefits of diversification at a fraction of the cost.

By definition, any mutual fund offers some degree of diversification, because every fund invests in many different stocks or bonds. But some funds are more diversified than others. For example, *sector funds,* which concentrate on investing in a single industry, are less diversified than most other stock funds. When economic trends favor that industry, the corresponding sector fund profits.

For example, during the late 1990s, sector funds that concentrate on the stock of Internet companies and other high-tech businesses have done very well. If and when high-tech industry flounders, however, the technology funds will, too. Thus, keeping all your money is one such fund would be a risky strategy.

Low entry cost

You can get started in mutual fund investing with relatively little money — a benefit when finances are tight, but you're mentally ready to roll with an investment experience.

When you buy shares of an individual stock, any purchase less than 100 shares is usually considered an *odd lot,* on which you must pay a high sales commission.

But a bundle of 100 shares of stock isn't easy for most investors to afford. If a stock is trading at (for example) $75 per share, 100 shares will cost $7,500 — a significant amount of money for most people.

By contrast, you can start investing in most mutual funds for just $1,000 to $2,000, and add to your investment later with even smaller amounts by sending a check to the fund company or arranging for automatic deductions from your checking account.)

If you have only a small amount of money to invest but are eager to get started in mutual funds, check out Table 3-1. This list, which is based on information provided by The Mutual Fund Education Alliance, gives you a sampling of fund companies and categories to consider when you're looking to invest $500 or less. You can request information on specific funds by contacting any broker, the fund companies themselves, or The Mutual Fund Education Alliance (www.mfea/com).

Table 3-1:   Finding an Investment Fit with $500 or Less

Fund Company	Fund Category	Co. Contact #
American Century	Aggressive Growth	800-345-2021; 816-640-7010
Babson Funds	Growth; Bond	800-422-2766
Berger Funds	Aggressive Growth; Growth; Growth and Income; International/Global; Balanced Equity	800-333-1001
Charles Schwab	Money Market	800-435-4000
Fidelity Investments	Growth; Growth and Income; Specialty/Sector; Bond	800-544-6666; 801-534-1910
Scudder Kemper	Growth and Income; Balanced/Equity; Bond	800-336-6923; 800-336-5140
TIAA-CREF	Bond; Growth; Growth and Income; International/Global; Money Market; Specialty/Sector	800-842-2733

Professional management

Mutual funds hire smart investment experts to manage your money, and they have access to extensive research into companies, economic conditions, and market trends. Most people would have a hard time keeping track of a large number of investments in many different businesses; staying on top of that financial activity is part of the daily routine for the research staff of a mutual fund.

Liquidity

Liquidity refers to the ease with which you can buy or sell an investment. Buying or selling a particular stock or bond, especially one held by relatively few people, may be difficult. If you need cash in an emergency, this obstacle to turning your investment into legal tender can cause inconvenience and may cost you money. By contrast, mutual fund shares can be cashed in quickly at any time by redeeming them with the managing company, usually at little or no cost.

Shareholder services

Many mutual fund companies offer a range of useful, sometimes valuable services to their customers. These may include

- Check-writing privileges
- Ability to invest, withdraw, or move money via mail, telephone, or the Internet
- Automatic investment via payroll deduction
- Record-keeping for filing your income tax return
- Access to research reports about companies, funds, and economic trends

A fund's prospectus tells you more about such services.

Disadvantages of Investing in Mutual Funds

Although mutual funds are tremendously varied, flexible, and convenient, they have disadvantages that you need to consider before investing.

Risks involving fund management

These days, mutual funds are among your safer investment options. Diversification, professional management, and the fraud-prevention exercised by the Security Exchange Commission and other regulatory bodies all help ensure that mutual funds stay relatively safe. Nonetheless, investing in mutual funds carries various kinds of risk that can impact your financial planning.

One risk that's inherent in the nature of mutual funds is the fact that you, the investor, have no control over what's being purchased for the portfolio. You are putting your money — and your investment fate — in the hands of the fund manager, which is why you need to study the track record of the fund company and the individual manager before you invest.

Making sure that you're giving your money to a reliable partner is important to your pocketbook and your peace of mind. I explain how to make sure you're selecting capable mutual fund managers in Chapters 7 and 8.

Another unpredictable challenge may arise when a fund's "star" manager retires or changes jobs, leaving the fund without his expertise or brilliance. For example, Peter Lynch was one of the most successful and famous mutual fund managers in the world for many years. Under his guidance, the Fidelity Magellan Fund grew into the largest mutual fund anywhere, with over \$72 billion in assets. Millions of investors poured money into Magellan, attracted largely by

Lynch's reputation and prestige. Since Lynch's retirement in 1990, however, Magellan has performed with far less success, despite the strong performance of the stock market overall.

If you're a fund investor, follow the financial news. Be aware when changes in the management of your funds occur. You may want to consider switching funds when the manager responsible for your fund's track record departs the scene.

Risk involving changes in the market

Even with expert management, however, the risk involved in mutual fund investing does not disappear. Sometimes, the stock or bond market as a whole may be in decline, and even smart investors are unable to make a profit. Such hard times are referred to as *bear markets.*

The opposite of a bear market is a time when the markets are steadily rising — *bull market.* Pessimistic investors are sometimes referred to as *bears,* while optimists are *bulls.* Now you understand the livestock references that you often hear scattered throughout financial news reports!

If you're a long-term investor, bear markets may not be a problem. You can probably wait until the market rebounds before selling your shares. A short-term investor, however, may get stuck with losses. Although you can't avoid risk altogether, you can choose money market mutual funds or other investments that don't tend to fluctuate dramatically, as I note in Chapter 1.

Unclear investment approach

Sometimes funds are managed in ways that contradict the image presented in advertising or promotion. A fund that is touted as a conservative fund — one that selects investments so as to minimize risk and volatility — may be managed in an aggressive manner, putting money into highly volatile small-company stocks, for example.

A fund that calls itself a stock fund may actually keep a sizeable portion of its investment money in cash or in short-term government bonds, which are considered equivalent to cash; thus, it may miss out on some of the gains enjoyed during a strong period for the stock market.

Tip

Instead of relying solely on advertising, press accounts, or the advice of a broker, always ask for a *prospectus* before investing in a fund. This is a detailed description of the fund and its investments, written according to government guidelines. Compare what you read in the prospectus with the sales pitch presented in ads or by a broker. If you feel there's a contradiction between them, don't hesitate to ask about it. (Chapter 7 contains more information about how to digest all the details in a prospectus, including the real clues to a fund's character.)

Lack of insurance for fund investments

Unlike your deposit in a bank, credit union, or savings and loan association (S&L), your investment in a mutual fund is not insured by the Federal Deposit Insurance Corporation or any other government agency. (Supervision of investment companies by the Security Exchange Commission and other organizations does not insure the value of your investment.) Therefore, when the fund invests in securities that rise and fall in value, you have the possibility of losing your initial investment.

In some states, mutual funds may be sold by banks and S&Ls or by brokerage companies associated with them and housed on the same premises. Read the fine print, and don't be confused. Although you may make a mutual fund investment over a counter in your local bank, your money will not be insured the way a bank deposit is. Walk, don't run, from any banker who implies the opposite.

Tax inefficiency

Another disadvantage to mutual funds is that stock funds (also called *equity* funds) are not very "tax-efficient." Here's how this inefficiency plays out in your overall investment picture: When you own individual stocks, you decide when to buy and sell them.

When you sell a stock that has increased in price, you receive a type of profit known as a *capital gain.* At the end of the year, you must pay taxes to the IRS on all the capital gains you enjoyed during that year. But with mutual funds, the schedule of stock purchases and sales is up to the fund manager — you don't have control of the timing.

Fortunately, there are funds managed specifically to minimize tax inefficiency. I explain how this works in Chapter 9.

Many stock investors carefully regulate their sales of stock so that they incur capital gains when the additional money is less burdensome to their tax situation. For example, a stock investor might choose to realize her capital gains during a year when her salary from work is smaller, thereby reducing her overall tax rate.

Mutual fund investing, however, means that you may receive capital gains distributions from the fund at any time. Of course, you end up paying taxes on these at the end of the year.

At tax time, mutual fund firms send out copies of Tax Form 1099-DIV to their mutual fund investors. The document details taxable earnings. Don't fail to report this income on your return; the fund company is also reporting it to the IRS, which will check for discrepancies.

If you are in a high tax bracket — that is, if your overall income is large enough to make your federal tax rate burdensome — and if you have a significant amount of money to invest in the stock market (say, $25,000 or more), you *may* want to consider investing in individual stocks rather than mutual funds so that you can better control the tax effects of your investments.

I tell you more about the tax implications of mutual fund investing in Chapter 9.

Uncertainty about redemption price

When you own an individual stock, you can choose to sell it at any time during the trading day (that is, while the stock market is in operation), and you will get the price that's current at the moment you sell. When the stock market, or a particular stock, is very volatile, your selling price can change significantly throughout the day.

For example, the stock of an individual company may start the trading day at a price of $40.00 per share, rise to $45.00 by the middle of the day, and then fall to $37.50 by the end of the day. A simple calculation shows how time can affect the amount of money you may make from selling 100 shares: from an early morning $4,000, to an afternoon $4,500, to a day's end $3,750.

When you want to redeem (that is, sell) shares of a mutual fund, the time of the day when you submit your request (by phone, fax, Internet, or mail) doesn't matter. Although the net asset value (NAV) of the fund (as I explain in Chapter 2) may rise and fall throughout the day, you always end up receiving a check based on the closing price for the end of the trading day (4 p.m. Eastern time).

If you want to be relatively certain of the NAV at which your shares will be redeemed, place your sale order at or near the end of the trading day. That way, you know that the price quoted over the phone will probably be the same, or almost the same, as that day's closing price.

No maturity dates

Another disadvantage of mutual funds relates specifically to bond funds — that is, funds that specialize in bonds rather than stocks or other investments. Typically, when you invest in an individual bond, you are given a *maturity date* — that is, the date when the loan represented by the bond comes due. On that date, you get back the amount you paid for the bond (the *principal*), plus interest. The return is certain, unless the company or the government body that issued the bond runs into financial difficulties.

An investment in a bond fund works differently. The fund manager is continually buying and selling bonds with a variety of maturity dates. Periodically, you receive a portion of the interest earned by the fund. However, no specific maturity date exists for your shares in the fund, and thus no certainty about the amount you can expect to receive when you decide to sell your shares. You may end up selling your shares in the fund for more or for less than you paid.

CHAPTER 4

LOOKING AT STOCK EQUITY FUNDS

IN THIS CHAPTER

- Sizing up stock funds

- Examining stock funds

- Picking the type of stock fund that's right for you

Mutual funds come in many flavors, and clever folks are inventing new, specialized types of funds all the time. Which kinds of funds are right for you? In this chapter, I explain some of the more popular types of funds and suggest which investors ought to be most interested in which fund types.

Defining Stock (Equity) Mutual Funds

Stock mutual funds (sometimes also called *equity* mutual funds) invest primarily in stocks (also called equities).

Although you can find many specific types of stock funds with widely varying risk and reward characteristics, stock funds in general outperform bond funds. Stock funds are top performers because they're invested in the stock market, which has proven, over many decades, to be the world's fastest-growing investment arena.

Over the past 20 years, the return of stock funds has been quite good — about 14.8% in average annual gain, including all kinds of profits (growth in net asset value, dividends, and capital gains).

However, a tradeoff is involved. The higher growth of stock funds comes with somewhat greater risk. Stock funds may rise or fall, depending on the behavior of the overall stock market, of particular industries, or of the specific companies selected by the fund manager. In a prolonged bear (declining) market, stock funds may even stagnate for a period of months or years.

The longer your investment horizon (that is, the more you are focused on long-term rather than short-term investment goals), the more appropriate stock funds are for your portfolio. If you expect to cash in your investment within the next three years, you should consider keeping all or most of your money in bond funds or other relatively safer investments.

Not all stock funds behave alike, as shown in Figure 4-1. Wide variations are possible among stock funds in terms of risk, volatility, and growth potential. The following sections highlight some common types of stock funds, with explanations of how each kind of fund can be expected to perform.

Figure 4-1: Sample annual returns for various fund categories.

Annual Returns

	1 year	5 year	10 year
Stock (Equity) Mutual Funds	11.98%	18.01%	15.75%
Index Funds	31.44%	26.47%	21.13%
Small Cap Funds	(9.49%)	17.34%	14.21%
Growth Funds	(25.15%)	20.49%	17.91%
Growth and Income Funds	(18.69%)	20.54%	17.30%
International Mutual Funds	(14.32%)	8.29%	9.48%

Index Funds

To understand index funds, you must first understand what a stock market index is.

A stock market *index* is a list of stocks whose combined performance is tracked by investors as an indication of the health of a particular portion of the economy.

Even people who know little or nothing about the stock market have heard of some of the more famous indexes and the companies they track—for example, the Dow Jones Industrial Average, the oldest and best-known index, tracks the stocks of 30 of America's bigger, more famous firms, including American Express, Coca-Cola, Walt Disney, McDonald's, and Wal-Mart Stores.

The value of the Dow is calculated by combining the share prices of all 30 companies according to a special formula. As the values of these companies rise and fall, the Dow rises and falls with them.

Because the Dow reflects the performance of the stock of only 30 companies, it can't accurately reflect the diversity of the entire U.S. economy — much less the world economy. So over the years, other indexes have been invented by various financial companies, each mirroring the performance of a different group of stocks:

- **The Standard and Poor's (S&P) 500 Index:** Tracks the performance of some 500 large U.S. companies. S&P 500 is often referred to as a "broader" index than the Dow because it's more inclusive and therefore reflects more general trends in American industry.

- **The Wilshire 5000 Index:** Tracks virtually the entire U.S. stock market.

- **The Russell 2000 Index:** Tracks smaller, fast-growing companies.

- **The Morgan Stanley Select Emerging Markets Index:** Tracks companies in developing regions of the world, such as South America, Southeast Asia, and Eastern Europe.

An *index fund* is a mutual fund that buys the stocks contained in a particular index. For example, the Vanguard Index Trust — the first index fund, founded in 1976 — owns shares of all the companies in the S&P 500. The investment objective of an index fund depends on the index being followed.

A broad index reflects changes in the overall economy, which usually moves more gradually than any single business sector. Thus, a broad index is usually less volatile than a more narrow one; and so, in general, the broader the index, the more conservative the fund. Index funds are available today based on every popular stock market index.

As you may imagine, managing an index fund is less challenging than managing most other fund types. The manager of an index fund is simply charged with buying and selling stocks to match those contained in its index. This style of fund management is sometimes called *passive investing*. By contrast, other funds are run by managers who must constantly make independent investment decisions; this is known as *active investing*.

Remember

Because passive investing calls for less complicated managerial decisions, the cost of running an index fund is less than with other fund types. Thus, investors in index funds generally incur lower management fees (see Chapter 6).

In general, index funds perform well; in fact, the majority of funds that are actively managed actually grow *less* quickly than such broad indexes as the S&P 500! "Beating the indexes" isn't an easy challenge, even for a highly skilled professional money manager. So index fund investing has become a particularly popular choice among investors who want to enjoy some of the strong growth possible in the stock market while minimizing the risks that go with active management.

Because passively managed funds trade less often than actively managed funds, index funds generate less capital gain income than most other funds (check out Chapter 2). This is a tax benefit for most investors, as explained in Chapter 9.

Small Cap Funds

Some stock mutual funds are characterized by the *market capitalization* of the companies whose shares they own. Market capitalization is the value that the stock market assigns to a company, derived by multiplying the stock price by the total number of shares.

For example, if a particular company's stock has a current price of $42 per share, and 10 million shares of stock are held by investors, the company's market capitalization would equal $42 × 10 million = $420 million. Theoretically, this is the purchase price to buy all the shares of the company on the open market.

A *small cap fund* specializes in companies with a relatively small market capitalization — usually below $1 billion. Some small cap funds focus on start-up companies, often in new or emerging industries such as high technology. Others focus on established companies that have plenty of room for growth. Office Depot, the popular chain of office supply stores, is a current example of a growing small cap company.

The smaller firms whose stock is owned by a small cap fund can be very profitable investments, but they can also be risky. If the company managers make a few mistakes — expanding too quickly, for example, or sinking too much money into an unproven technology — the firm may go bankrupt. Thus, the manager of a small cap fund needs to have a shrewd sense of business judgment in order to separate the truly promising small firms from those that are shaky.

You may want to put a portion of your investment money into a small cap fund — but not all of it. For example, if you invest 20% of your savings in a small cap fund, you have the opportunity to enjoy rapid growth if the fund does well, without running the risk of losing your whole retirement or college portfolio if the fund runs into bad luck.

Large Cap Funds

A *large cap fund* specializes in stocks with a market value of more than $5 billion. Such a fund focuses on large, well-established companies, which tend to have lower risk than small companies. Large firms also often provide dividend income, which smaller and newer firms rarely do (see Chapter 2). Examples of large cap companies are IBM and General Motors. (They are also known as *blue chip* stocks, named after the most expensive chips used for gambling games like poker.)

As always, the benefits of large cap funds come with trade-offs. Although a large cap fund is relatively low-risk, growth is likely to be steady, but slow in most economic circumstances. A big, old company like General Motors has a well-established position in the auto marketplace, and the number of cars sold in the United States or the world is probably not going to double or triple in the next five years.

By contrast, sales could grow that quickly in a brand-new industry such as biotechnology. Thus, a large cap fund is a good choice for a more conservative investor, or for that portion of your portfolio that you don't want to take chances with. (These generalizations don't always hold true. At times, large cap funds actually grow more quickly than small cap funds. But such times are the exception rather than the rule.)

Mid Cap Funds

As its name suggests, a *mid cap stock fund* (also known as medium cap) falls between small cap and large cap funds, usually owning shares in companies that have market capitalization between $1 billion and $5 billion. Some business sectors that contain mid cap stocks are utility companies (such as oil, gas, and electric companies), service companies (such as retail chains), and some technology companies.

Mid cap fund performance tends to fall between that of small and large companies, too: mid caps face less risk of failure than small cap stocks, but have better earnings potential than large cap stocks.

Growth Funds

A *growth fund* is a stock fund managed primarily in pursuit of capital gains — that is, most of the profit sought by the manager takes the form of higher share prices rather than dividends paid. The manager of a growth fund is interested in finding industries that are rapidly expanding due to economic, business, or social trends and individual companies that are managed so effectively that they are growing quickly.

A growth fund may invest in stocks of large, small, or mid cap companies. The success of the fund depends heavily on the expertise of its manager and his ability to pick winners from among the many companies competing in a particular industry.

For example, one industry for which many economists predict a bright future over the next two decades is pharmaceuticals, which manufacture drugs, medicines, and other health-related products. As the large baby boom generation born in the 1940s and 1950s ages, their need for medical care is likely to increase, and pharmaceutical companies are positioned to enjoy growing sales and profits.

The manager of a growth fund probably wants to follow the pharmaceutical industry closely. However, to be successful, the fund manager also needs to identify the individual companies in the industry whose stock is likely to perform best.

Key to successful fund management is staying informed about the management of the leading pharmaceutical firms — Pfizer, Merck, Glaxo, Lilly, and others — and listening for news about breakthrough medicines in development at each company.

The growth fund manager who can accurately guess which firms are destined to do well in the years to come will make profitable stock selections, and investors in his fund will benefit accordingly.

A growth fund is usually a good investment for the long-term investor. For example, if you're investing for a retirement that is 20 years or more in the future, you may want to put half or more of your investment money into a growth fund, which should benefit from upward trends in the economy during the coming decades.

Aggressive Growth Funds

If a growth fund seeks companies that can grow at 60 miles per hour, an *aggressive growth fund* is like a race-car driver. The manager of such a fund buys stocks she thinks have the most exciting growth possibilities, including small cap stocks, stocks of companies that are developing new technologies, and stocks in firms whose business is likely to double or triple within a few years.

In pursuit of higher returns, aggressive growth funds take greater risks and are subject to greater volatility. If you invest in an aggressive growth fund, your money may shrink by 50% one year and grow by 100% the next. Don't pick this kind of fund unless you can handle a financial roller-coaster ride.

An aggressive growth fund also may use financial techniques that involve more risk. One example is the use of *options* and other so-called *derivative instruments*. When an investor buys an option, he buys the right to buy or sell a stock (or other security) at a prespecified price at some time in the future.

In effect, an option is a bet that the price of a security will move in a specific direction, up or down. If the investor bets right, the profits can be large; if he bets wrong, the losses can be just as large.

If you suspect that a mutual fund is being managed in a high-risk fashion, study the prospectus carefully. If the document indicates that the fund manager is investing in options, futures, or other derivative instruments, make sure you understand the degree and nature of the financial risk involved. And don't invest more money than you can afford to lose. Gambling a little can be fun — but not with the money you're relying on for retirement or your kids' education.

Growth and Income Funds

A *growth and income fund* is generally lower in risk than a growth fund. Such a fund invests in companies that have good growth potential but also pay dividends to their investors (more on the subject in Chapter 2).

The fact that the fund profits in at least two ways from its investments cushions volatility, making it more of an "all-weather" fund than the more uncertain growth fund. This type of fund is less volatile because the dividends keep coming even if the stock price goes down.

In most cases, stock dividends represent a relatively minor portion of the profits you make from a mutual fund. In a recent year, for example, stocks listed in the S&P 500 Index paid an average dividend of about 1.3%. (Thus, if you owned a share of stock priced at $75 which paid the average dividend, you'd receive, in the course of the year, checks totaling $0.97 per share — not a huge sum by any standard.) On the other hand, the average dividend yield from an aggressive growth fund in the same year was just 0.2%.

Obviously, if the security of knowing that dividends are rolling in is important to you, stay with a growth and income fund rather than seeking aggressive growth.

International Mutual Funds

More and more investors today are seeking investment opportunities outside the United States. This makes economic sense. Although the United States is still a dynamic, growing nation, it's also a mature country, whose business, social, and economic structures are largely in place.

By contrast, some other regions of the world have the potential of growing very quickly in the years ahead, as they try to rapidly catch up to the United States in terms of industry and consumer spending.

Investors seeking growth opportunities should consider putting at least part of their money into *international* or *global mutual funds,* which specialize in foreign investments.

Naturally, international investing involves many complexities. Someone who invests in foreign stocks has to worry about foreign economies, interest rates, tax laws, political conditions, and business practices. But with an international mutual fund, the fund manager does all the research — and the worrying — for you. You gain exposure to overseas opportunities without the headaches.

One type of risk that is unique to international investing is *currency risk.* When you put $1,000 in an international fund, you are, in effect, buying foreign currency, because the fund has to change your dollars into German marks, Russian rubles, Indian rupees, or some other foreign money before it can be invested.

As you know, the *exchange rate* between U.S. currency and other currencies is constantly in flux, based mainly on changes in the world and local economies. One day, the U.S. dollar may be worth 110 Japanese yen; the next day, it may rise to 150 yen. When the U.S. dollar is up, the relative value of your foreign holdings will go down. On the other hand, when the dollar drops, your foreign currencies go up, which is an added benefit to your portfolio.

To minimize the dangers of currency risk, try to limit your international investing to long-term money — funds you won't need to withdraw quickly. By exercising patience, you can wait for a favorable movement in currency values before you sell your shares. Also, try to diversify your international holdings. Pick funds that invest in several international economies rather than just one. Currency losses in one country can offset profits in another.

International funds include funds that invest in specific countries, such as England or Japan, as well as regional funds. The term *global* is generally used to describe funds that invest in U.S. companies as well as foreign ones.

Emerging Market Mutual Funds

An *emerging market mutual fund* is a type of international fund that invests in so-called emerging markets, such as Latin America, Africa, Southeast Asia, the Middle East, and Eastern Europe.

Emerging market funds are relatively risky for several reasons. Currency values are often volatile, making currency risk greater than with the developed nations of Europe or Asia; political problems are more likely, which can affect the economic prospects of a country and therefore the value of your investments. In addition, stock markets in emerging nations are usually less liquid because you have fewer investors looking for stocks to buy.

You can make big returns from an emerging market fund, especially if your fund's manager is fortunate enough to pick countries or companies that are on the verge of successful business breakthroughs.

But the potential for large losses is always present. Consider investing part of your portfolio in an emerging market fund, but only a portion that you can afford to lose.

Sector Funds

A *sector fund* specializes in stocks from a particular industry. The manager of a sector fund is an expert on the companies in that industry, its long-term growth prospects, and the business and social trends that are likely to affect it. Consider investing in a sector fund if you feel a particular business has special potential for success.

Table 4-1 shows the investment results for three recent years in a number of the more popular business sectors covered by sector funds. (The returns are shown as percent increases or decreases in the fund's value.)

Notice that the results vary widely by industry, and also that they are quite volatile. Utility funds, for example, which invest in water companies, power companies, phone companies, and the like, lost significant money in 1994, performed extremely well in 1995, and then had only mediocre performance during 1996.

Table 4-1:   Yearly Total Returns of Selected Sector Fund Groups

(Source: Lipper Analytical Services Inc.)

Sector	1994	1995	1996
Gold-Oriented	-12.2	2.4	7.5
Environmental	-7.8	27.7	18.5
Financial Services	-2.7	41.5	28.0
Health/Biotechnology	4.3	47.2	13.4
Natural Resources	-3.6	17.1	32.4
Real Estate	-2.9	13.9	30.9
Science and Technology	16.4	39.5	19.1
Utilities	-9.1	27.4	9.9

Remember

Choose a sector fund only if you're prepared to live with similar ups and downs.

CHAPTER 5

FINDING OUT ABOUT BOND FUNDS AND BALANCED FUNDS

IN THIS CHAPTER

- Defining bond funds
- Investing in both stocks and bonds with balanced funds

Bond funds and balanced funds are two types of specialized funds that may fit your investment personality. In this chapter, I explain bond and balanced funds and suggest when each type of fund is right for you.

Exploring Bond (Fixed Income) Funds

Bond funds invest in many kinds of bonds, which represent IOUs from business or government agencies to which money has been lent. The primary objective of a bond fund is income from the interest paid on the loans. Whereas the value of a stock constantly changes in ways that are often unpredictable, the interest income on a bond is predetermined and can be relied upon, unless the business or government agency runs into serious financial difficulties. Thus, bonds are sometimes called *fixed income securities,* and bond funds may be referred to as *fixed income funds.*

Because bond funds are usually less volatile and lower-risk than stock funds, they are often chosen by investors whose main objective is safety. Therefore, consider bond funds for short-term investment goals. In addition, many investors like to keep a portion of their money in bonds at all times, as a way of guarding against large, unexpected shifts in the stock market. (I talk about this strategy in more detail in Chapter 8.)

Money market funds

A *money market mutual fund* invests in short-term bonds issued by the U.S. government, large corporations, states and local governments, banks, and other rock-solid institutions.

As I explain in Chapter 1, a money market fund is considered a conservative investment with little possibility of losing money; in fact, many investors and financial experts refer to money market funds as a *cash equivalent,* almost as safe and liquid as money in the bank.

Because money market investments are short-term (that is, bonds that are to be paid off within a few weeks or months), they closely reflect current interest rates. Most money market mutual funds are currently earning about 4% interest (computed as an annual growth rate).

During the early 1980s, when inflation and interest rates were both very high, money market funds earned over 10% annually. Such growth is unlikely to return unless economic conditions change dramatically.

You can invest in money market funds through a mutual fund company or a bank. In most cases, banks pay slightly lower interest rates than do mutual fund companies. Also remember that your money market investment through a bank is not federally insured, unlike ordinary bank deposits.

A money market fund is a good place to keep money that you may need in a hurry. It's also a handy parking place for money that you plan to invest somewhere, but you just haven't decided exactly where.

For example, Joanne gets a larger-than-expected end-of-year bonus from the company where she works — $2,500. She can deposit the bonus check in a money market fund managed by a mutual fund companies. It will immediately begin earning about 4% interest. Over the next month or two, Joanne can take her time to research other investment opportunities. If she then decides to invest the bonus in a growth fund (for example), she can move the money from the money market fund into the growth fund simply by placing a call to the mutual fund company.

Municipal bond funds

A *municipal bond* is an IOU issued by a state, country, city, or other local government, often designed to raise money for a particular purpose. A county may issue bonds, for example, in order to borrow money to build a new airport, fix local roads, or expand a park. A *municipal bond fund* invests in a portfolio of such bonds.

Municipal bonds often pay slightly lower interest rates than other government or corporate bonds. Their popularity stems from their tax advantages. The interest from most municipal bonds is exempt from federal income taxes. Furthermore, you don't pay state taxes on municipal bonds issued within your own state; and, if you pay local income taxes (as residents of New York City do, for example), you can even find *triple tax-exempt bonds* that are free from local income taxes, too.

To decide whether a municipal bond fund makes sense for you, figure out what tax bracket you are in. (This will depend on your annual income as well as the number and kind of tax exemptions and deductions you enjoy. Any tax advisor can help you determine this.) Then refer to Table 5-1, which shows how the income from a tax-free municipal bond fund would compare to the after-tax income you'd receive from an ordinary fund.

For example, suppose you are in the 28% federal tax bracket. If you can get a 6% tax-free yield from a municipal bond fund, that would be equivalent to an 8.33% yield on which you must pay taxes. This table can help you compare a municipal bond fund investment with a taxable investment and decide which is a better deal for you.

Table 5-1:   Taxable Equivalent Yields

Tax Bracket	4%	5%	6%	7%	8%
15%	4.71	5.88	7.06	8.24	9.41
28%	5.56	6.94	8.33	9.72	11.11
31%	5.80	7.25	8.70	10.14	11.59
36%	6.25	7.81	9.38	10.94	12.50
39.6%	6.62	8.28	9.93	11.59	13.25

Corporate bond funds

A *corporate bond fund* invests in debt issued by companies that need to raise money. Such bonds are rated for their safety by Standard & Poor's and Moody's, two companies that specialize in examining the finances of companies and determining whether they are likely to be able to pay off their debts in a timely fashion. (They are also the same organizations that invented some of the stock indexes I refer to in Chapter 4.)

Standard & Poor's and Moody's rate bonds using letter grades — S&P's AAA and Moody's Aaa represent the highest possible grades. In general, investors want to invest in bond funds that hold bonds rated in the four highest categories: AAA ("triple A"), AA, A, and BBB, according to S&P or Aaa, Aa, A, and Baa, according to Moody's. The companies that issue these bonds are unlikely to go bankrupt or to fail to repay their debts, so the risk is fairly low. However, corporate bond funds are still slightly riskier than government bonds, so corporate bonds pay slightly better interest to compensate.

One type of corporate bond for most investors to avoid is the so-called *high-yield bond*, also known as a *junk bond*. As the latter name implies, such bonds are very risky. They're offered by companies that are small, sometimes struggling, and prone to great shifts of fortune, either up or down.

Fortunes have been made by high-yield bond investors — and also lost. If you're offered the opportunity to invest in a high-yield bond fund, examine it cautiously, and only invest money that you can afford to lose. It may happen.

Because investors are wary of high-yield or junk bonds, some brokers or other bond funds salespeople may try to sell you a high-yield bond fund without identifying it as such. If you are offered shares in a bond fund with an interest rate two or three percentage points higher than other funds you are considering, be careful! Chances are that the risk associated with the fund is very high, even if the salesperson doesn't reveal the fact.

Learning about Balanced Funds

A *balanced fund* owns both stocks and bonds. It's a conservative type of fund investment, one that attempts to make it easy for investors to enjoy some of the safety of bonds along with the growth potential of stocks through a single investment.

The typical balanced fund is 60% invested in stocks and 40% in bonds. Its investment objective is to conserve principal (that is, avoid losing any of the money invested), pay current income (that is, dividends), and achieve long-term growth.

If you're a brand-new investor, a balanced fund can be an easy, safe choice. If you have a little more experience, consider creating your own "balanced" fund by dividing your money between stock and bond funds of your choice.

By selecting funds that closely fit your own investment goals, you're likely to achieve better results than you can get from a prepackaged balanced fund.

Figure 5-1 shows a comparison of average annual total returns of bond and balanced fund categories, covering both short-term (1 year) and longer-term (5 and 10 year) performance. (Be sure to base your investment research on current performance information.)

Figure 5-1:   Sample annual returns for various funds, including balanced funds.

Annual Returns

	1 year	5 year	10 year
Fixed Income (Bond) Funds	9.56%	8.00%	10.19%
Money Market Funds	5.57%	5.62%	5.98%
Municipal Bond Funds	6.63%	5.67%	8.23%
Corporate Bond Funds	8.22%	6.95%	9.38%
Balanced Funds	14.83%	14.73%	14.09%

CHAPTER 6
UNCOVERING MUTUAL FUND FEES AND EXPENSES

IN THIS CHAPTER

- Comparing load and no-load funds
- Evaluating your investment expenses
- Looking out for 12b-1 fees
- Tuning in to turnover

Although mutual funds provide many benefits to the individual investor, these benefits aren't free for the asking. Buying and owning a mutual fund involves costs, which can greatly affect the profitability of a given investment. Fortunately, these expenses are evident if you study the fund's prospectus, so you never have to make an uninformed decision about what costs you're willing to carry.

Load versus No-Load Funds

Soon after you begin reading about the world of mutual funds, you're sure to encounter the distinction between *load* and *no-load funds*. The difference between them is important.

Load funds

A *load* is a sales charge or commission payable to the person who sells you a mutual fund. A *load fund* is a mutual fund on which such fees are charged.

Typically, a financial professional sells a load fund. Some load funds are sold by *full-service brokers* — salespeople who advise you on your investment choices, provide you with brochures and research reports, and pocket a commission in return for their work. Financial planners, bankers, insurance agents, and other financial professionals also sell load funds.

All load funds carry attached sales commissions, usually representing about 5% of your investment. For example, if you invest $1,000 in a certain load stock fund with a 5.75% sales charge, $57.50 comes off the top to pay the broker. The remaining $942.50 is your investment in the mutual fund itself.

Redemption fees

Instead of up-front sales charges, some load funds charge a *redemption fee.* With this kind of load, you pay a fee when you cash out of the fund by selling your shares. The size of the redemption fee depends on the fund you are invested in; each fund has its own fee structure, often on a sliding scale, so that the redemption fee decreases the longer you hold the fund.

For example, a typical redemption fee structure provides that, if you redeem your mutual fund shares within a six-year window, you can expect to pay anywhere from 6% to 1% — 6% during the first year, 5% during the second year, and so on. The redemption fee drops off at the seventh year. (By design, the fee structure encourages you to hold on to your investment for a longer time, which benefits the fund company.)

Carefully study the sales brochure or prospectus (Chapter 7) for any fund you're thinking of investing in. Make sure you understand the nature, size, and structure of any load charge. Some load funds impose up-front sales charges; others include redemption fees; others levy annual commissions for as long as you own the fund; and still others impose various combinations of these charges. Read the fine print so you won't be blindsided by unanticipated expenses.

No-load funds

A *no-load fund* charges no sales commission. Typically, the mutual fund firm that sponsors the fund is the investor's source for this kind of fund. These firms often sponsor entire families of no-load funds, each with a different investment objective, philosophy, and style.

Some of the better-known mutual fund families, including T. Rowe Price, Fidelity, Janus, and Vanguard, offer a wide array of no-load funds, one of which is likely to be an appropriate and attractive investment for you.

When you invest in a no-load fund, you skip the middleman — the sales agent — and therefore save the money that would otherwise go to pay his commission. You don't have to meet with or speak to a broker or salesperson; instead, you call the mutual fund company, ask for an application and informational brochures about their funds, and then send in a completed application form with your check. If you invest $1,000, the entire amount begins working for you, with no deduction for any load or commission.

Is there any significant downside to choosing a no-load fund? Not really. Some investors prefer load funds because they like having an ongoing relationship with a broker or other financial professional who can advise them from time to time.

By contrast, with a no-load fund, the investor is on her own; she can call the fund company to make transactions or to request publications, but she can count on speaking to a different representative every time she calls.

Remember

The investment performance of load and no-load funds is the subject of many research studies. In virtually every study, no significant difference is apparent. In other words, investors who paid sales commissions of 5% or more for load funds did *not* enjoy noticeably better investment results.

Because you can invest your money with equal profit in either a load or a no-load fund, why not save some of your hard-earned cash by considering only no-load funds for your portfolio? (But before deciding, consider the impact of 12b-1 fees, which I explain later in this chapter. These particular fees may tip the scales against certain no-load funds.)

Annual Operating Expenses

Of course, (almost) no good thing is free. All mutual funds have associated expenses — even no-load funds (see Figure 6-1). Before choosing any fund, learn about the costs you can expect to pay for the investment expertise and services the fund provides.

You can find the *annual operating expenses* of any fund described and estimated in the fund's prospectus. These expenses may include management fees, administrative costs, and 12b-1 fees, all of which I explain in this chapter. These fees are generally deducted automatically from your account and shown when you receive your regular account statement in the mail, so you don't have to worry about sending in a check.

Some funds are naturally more expensive to operate than others. A fund that invests in international stocks or small company stocks tends to be more expensive than average, because research costs are likely to be higher in these areas.

By contrast, an index fund that simply tracks the performance of a preselected bundle of stocks generally has lower expenses and therefore can save you money when you invest. However, the fact that a particular fund has relatively higher expenses need not deter you from investing in it. A high investment return may more than make up for the annual expenses charged.

Figure 6-1: Typical fees and expenses of a fund.

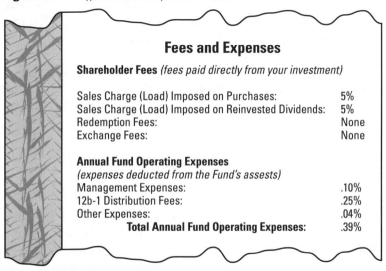

Fees and Expenses

Shareholder Fees *(fees paid directly from your investment)*

Sales Charge (Load) Imposed on Purchases:	5%
Sales Charge (Load) Imposed on Reinvested Dividends:	5%
Redemption Fees:	None
Exchange Fees:	None

Annual Fund Operating Expenses
(expenses deducted from the Fund's assests)

Management Expenses:	.10%
12b-1 Distribution Fees:	.25%
Other Expenses:	.04%
Total Annual Fund Operating Expenses:	.39%

Management fees

Management fees cover the fund company's management expenses — the work of lawyers and accountants, the cost of maintaining books and records, money spent complying with government regulations and disclosure rules, research expenses, and the salary of the fund manager, among other costs. The amount varies from fund to fund and from one type of fund to another.

Management fees are usually lower on money market mutual funds and other bond funds and higher on most types of equity funds because of the greater complexity of the investment decisions.

Management fees are usually the single largest portion of a fund's annual expenses, averaging between 0.5% and 1.0% of the fund's assets.

Administrative costs

Administrative costs may include a variety of expenses.

Shareholder service fees, sometimes referred to as *transfer agent service fees,* are typical administrative costs. The transfer agent maintains records of your ownership of the fund's shares. When you open an account, the transfer agent records that transaction. If you transfer money into or out of the fund, the agent records this activity. The agent also handles your redemption requests when you want to cash in all or part of your investment. And if the fund company distributes dividends or capital gains to investors, the transfer agent records that transaction.

Mutual fund companies offer other shareholder services, the cost of which is included in the same set of fees. When you call the fund company to set up an account, you talk to a representative; similarly, when you request information about a fund or receive an annual report in the mail, a fund employee must handle these services. Such expenses also come out of shareholder service fees.

Custodial fees are another type of fee included in the annual operating expenses listed in a fund's prospectus. When you invest in a mutual fund, you're buying stocks or bonds that must be handled by a third party — a *custodian.* The custodian holds the stock for you, provides ownership records to the mutual fund company, and handles various kinds of internal paperwork.

The custodian also tracks the action if a particular stock *splits* — that is, if the company issuing the stock decides to convert (say) 100 shares trading at $120 per share into 200 shares trading at $60 per share. (Companies sometimes do this in order to keep their per-share price fairly low and affordable.) The custodian handles the administrative work caused by stock splits.

For most domestic funds, custodial fees are usually not high. For funds that invest in foreign stocks, custodial fees can be substantial because of the complications of investing in foreign countries.

The expense ratio

One handy way to measure the relative cost of investing in a particular fund is by looking at its *expense ratio.* This figure, which appears in the fee table section of the fund's prospectus (see Chapter 7), is the amount that each investor can expect to pay for fund expenses each year, stated as a percentage of the money invested.

The expense ratio includes administrative costs and management fees but *not* sales charges (loads) or 12b-1 fees, which I explain in the following sections. Thus, the expense ratio provides you with a useful, though partial, picture of the costs involved in investing in a fund.

The average stock fund has an expense ratio of about 1.4%; for bond funds, the average is under 1.0%. A ratio higher than this may or may not be justifiable, depending on the kind of fund you are considering. Table 6-1 shows median expense ratios for some common types of funds.

Table 6-1:   Median Expense Ratios for Selected Fund Types

Fund Type	Median Expense Ratio (Given as a Percentage of Invested Funds)
Global	1.91
Sector	1.84
Aggressive growth	1.55
Growth and income	1.32
Bond (fixed income)	0.94
Municipal bond	0.89
Money market	0.67
S&P 500 index	0.37

12b-1 fees

A *12b-1 fee,* also known as a *marketing* or *distribution fee,* is an alternative way to pay the salesperson who sells the fund's shares and who may provide assistance and advice to the investor. 12b-1 fees may also defray advertising and other marketing expenses of the mutual fund company.

Any fund can establish a 12b-1 fee, although not all do. When 12b-1 fees exist, they generally range between 0.25% and 1.0% annually. By law, the fee can be no higher than 1 percentage point of the fund's average net assets per year.

A mutual fund that charges no sales load and charges 12b-1 fees of 0.25% or less is considered a no-load fund. However, if the 12b-1 fee is greater than 0.25%, the fund qualifies as a load fund.

Naturally, the lower the 12b-1 fees charged by a fund, the better. In general, no-load funds are a better bargain than load funds. However, you may find that, in some instances, a load fund may actually be a better buy than a fund with a heavy 12b-1 fee.

Suppose you're considering a fund with a modest front-end load (say, less than 5%). Because the front-end load is a one-time payment, while 12b-1 fees are an ongoing annual charge, the front-end load may end up costing you less, especially if you plan to keep your investment for a long time.

In effect, the existence of 12b-1 fees gives the investor a choice of whether to pay sales expenses later or up-front. Look closely at 12b-1 fees before making an investment decision — they may influence you to choose one fund over another.

The cost of turnover

Another cost of investing that doesn't show up in the expense ratio of a fund is the cost of *turnover.* Turnover is the rate at which a fund buys and sells investments. A turnover rate of 100% means that, on average, the fund manager buys and sells stocks or bonds with a value equivalent to that of the entire investment portfolio each year.

Every time the fund manager buys or sells a stock or bond, she incurs expenses — brokerage commissions and other administrative costs. The higher the turnover rate, the more frequent trading of securities the manager is engaged in, and the higher the trading costs. Over time, high turnover can be a significant drag on the profits of a fund.

You can find the fund's turnover rate in the prospectus (see Chapter 7). The least actively managed funds, such as an index fund, may have a very low turnover rate of just 5% to 10%. A very actively managed fund may have a turnover rate of 500% or more, meaning that each security in the fund is held, on average, for just about one-fifth of a year — 10 weeks or so — before being sold.

In general, turnover rates of less than 30% are considered low; 30% to 100% is average; over 100% is high.

If every other comparative point is equal, choose a fund with a lower turnover rate because more efficient fund management is likely to earn you greater profits in the long run.

RESEARCHING A MUTUAL FUND

IN THIS CHAPTER

- Matching investment goals with fund categories
- Finding high-performance funds
- Evaluating fund management
- Reading the fund prospectus

With thousands of mutual funds available today, you can easily feel overwhelmed when it comes to choosing one, two, or a few for your investment dollars. You can get off to a good start by knowing what you are trying to achieve by investing.

As I suggest in Chapter 1, the new investor can begin by listing his or her financial goals and deciding whether they are mainly long-term goals, short-terms goals, or a mixture of both. When you know your investment objectives, you can focus on specific types of funds, narrowing the universe from which you have to choose.

Matching Goals with Fund Categories

The following checklist contains some specific suggestions that can help you decide which types of funds may best suit your personal situation and goals:

- If your investment goals are mainly long-term, consider stock (equity) funds.

■ If your investment goals are mainly short-term, consider bond (fixed income) funds, especially money-market funds.

■ If you feel able to tolerate a relatively high degree of risk, consider growth funds, aggressive growth funds, emerging market funds, or mid cap and small cap funds.

■ If minimizing risk is important to you, consider bond funds (including corporate bond funds), balanced funds, growth and income funds, or large cap funds.

■ If you want to target specific regions or industries you think will grow, consider international or sector funds.

■ If you want to minimize the costs of investing, consider index funds.

■ If you want to minimize the taxes on your investment profits, consider municipal bond funds.

You can find more details on each of these fund types in Chapters 4 and 5.

Obviously, overlap exists among these various personal goals. A single investor — call him Matthew for the sake of illustration — may have two or three different yet complementary investment preferences.

For example, say he wants to invest for the long-term goal of retirement, minimize risk, and minimize the tax bite on his investment profits. In light of these three preferences, Matthew may want to consider more than one category of funds, looking for the fund type that offers a comfortable balance among different factors. So zeroing in on one category of fund isn't necessarily an obvious or easy process. The checklist can help you begin the process of sorting out the possibilities.

Finding High-Performing Funds

After you decide which categories of funds are likely to be best for you, you can begin to narrow your choices still further.

One way to start is by looking at the track record of a wide selection of funds in a particular category. Sources abound for this information.

Magazines that deal with personal finance and investing topics, such as *Money, Smart Money,* and *Kiplinger's Personal Finance Magazine,* run periodic special reports showing comparative investment results for hundreds of mutual funds. The publications usually group the funds by categories, so you can quickly zero in on growth funds, index funds, municipal bond funds, or any other fund type of interest to you.

Similar reports appear periodically in business magazines like *Business Week* and *Forbes,* in *The Wall Street Journal,* and in the business sections of many local newspapers. Visit your local library and ask a librarian to help you locate the most recent mutual fund issues of your favorite financial periodical or check out the publication online. The data you need ought to be easy to find. (The Resource Center appearing later in this book lists many sources of mutual fund information you're sure to find helpful.)

Be sure to compare the one-year, three-year, five-year, and ten-year annualized returns for funds in the specific type or types of funds you are considering (see Figure 7-1). Look for consistently strong results. The fund that amassed huge profits over the past 12 months may have done poorly in previous years, suggesting that next year's performance may lag again.

A better bet is a fund that shows an above-average performance year-in and year-out for the past five years or more. In

Chapter 7, I give you more suggestions about how to evaluate the track record of a particular mutual fund.

Figure 7-1: A sample Performance Report.

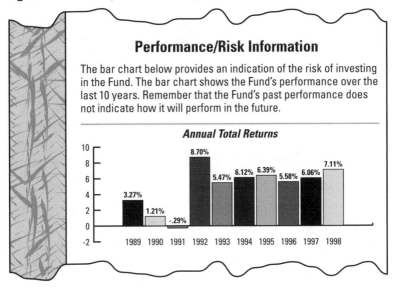

Performance/Risk Information

The bar chart below provides an indication of the risk of investing in the Fund. The bar chart shows the Fund's performance over the last 10 years. Remember that the Fund's past performance does not indicate how it will perform in the future.

Annual Total Returns

Evaluating Fund Management

By studying the track records of funds in the categories you're interested in, you can identify a handful of strong candidates to focus on even more closely. The next step is to examine the management of those funds, looking for signs of strength and weakness that may guide an investment decision.

Several firms, including Morningstar, Value Line, Lipper Analytical, and Wiesenberger, specialize in monitoring and tracking mutual funds and publishing reports on their findings. Most public libraries subscribe to at least one of the information services offered by these firms, and with the help of a librarian you can locate a wealth of information on the management styles and strengths of most mutual funds.

Below are some of the questions to ask about any fund that you are seriously considering buying. Information services like those provided by Morningstar, Value Line, and so on can provide the answers.

Who is the fund manager? How long has he or she managed the fund? How does the growth record of the fund under his or her management compare to that of other funds?

In general, you want the manager to have a record of at least five years with the fund company, preferably ten or more. If the manager has only been with the firm for two years, his track record is too short to be truly meaningful; any success the fund is currently enjoying may be due more to the efforts of his predecessor.

Information about fund managers often is readily available in the financial press. A few superstar fund managers, such as Mark Mobius, the international investment guru of the Templeton Funds, are almost as widely covered in the media as top basketball players or movie stars.

Check online or in any index of newspapers and magazines (available at your local library) for articles about or interviews with the managers of the funds you are considering. You may be able to locate one or more profiles in which the fund manager offers his investment philosophy, explains his successes and failures, and indicates some of his strategies for the months and years to come.

Do the investments currently held by the fund match the fund's stated objectives?

Fund management may not exactly match an advertised description. Some funds touted in advertising as low-risk or conservative investments actually include derivatives and other risky holdings in their portfolios.

Other funds whose names imply "stock" or "equity" may maintain a large portion of their holdings in cash-equivalent investments such as short-term bonds. So you can't assume that the name of a fund offers a fair description of its investment approach.

In order to determine whether the fund manager is investing according to the fund's stated investment objective, you may want to look at a breakdown of the fund's holdings.

Some mutual fund tracking firms offer these breakdowns; you can find similar data in the fund's prospectus (see "Reading the Fund Prospectus"). By looking at the current holdings of the fund, you can gauge how much is in stocks or in bonds and what portions of the fund are invested in various categories of companies — small cap versus large cap stocks, foreign stocks, high-tech businesses, blue chip companies, and so on (as I explain in Chapter 4). If you sense a discrepancy between the stated objective of the fund and the kind of securities that the fund actually holds, you may want to question the clarity and consistency of the fund's management.

The Morningstar Mutual Fund reports also feature a *style box*, which analyzes and describes the investment style used by the fund manager in the past. (See Figure 7-2.) From this box, you can tell whether the manager generally invests in small, mid (medium), or large cap stocks, and whether his preference is for companies geared toward growth (that is, rapid increase in company size and profits), value (that is, slow but steady growth and reliable income), or a blend of the two. This descriptive box provides a quick way to predict how the manager is likely to invest in the present and future. You want to feel comfortable with the direction the fund manager generally takes before sending your money to him for investment.

Figure 7-2: Stock and bond style boxes show investment strategies for various funds.

Stock Style Box

Risk	Investment Style			Median Market Capitalization
	Value	Blend	Growth	
Low ◯	Large cap Value	Large cap Blend	Large cap Growth	Large
Moderate ◯	Medium cap Value	Medium cap Blend	Medium cap Growth	Medium
High ◯	Small cap Value	Small cap Blend	Small cap Growth	Small

Within the stock style box grid, nine possible combinations exist ranging from large cap value for the safest funds to small cap growth for the riskiest.

Bond Style Box

Risk	Duration			Quality
	Short	Intermediate	Long	
Low ◯	Short-term High Quality	Interm-term High Quality	Long-term High Quality	High
Moderate ◯	Short-term Medium Quality	Interm-term Medium Quality	Long-term Medium Quality	Medium
High ◯	Short-term High Quality	Interm-term Low Quality	Long-term Low Quality	Low

Within the bond box grid, nine possible combinations exist, ranging from short duration or maturity/high quality for the safest funds to long duration or maturity/low quality for the riskiest.

How do the fund's fees and expenses compare to others in the fund category?

As I cover in Chapter 6, the sales charges, annual expenses, 12b-1 fees, and other costs associated with mutual funds vary widely from fund to fund. Look carefully at these charges and compare them from one fund to another. Be sure that you're aware of the expenses you're going to be responsible for, and factor them into your expectations of investment profit.

You may want to eliminate from consideration any fund with unusually high fees or expenses — unless its investment performance demonstrates consistently better results than other funds in the same category.

Reading the Fund Prospectus

The fund prospectus is a legal document that must contain specific information about a mutual fund. The prospectus informs potential investors about the fund's goals, fees, and expenses, and its investment objectives and degree of risk, as well as information on how to buy and sell shares.

You can obtain a prospectus directly from the fund company or from a broker, financial planner, or other financial professional. After you narrow your fund choices to a handful of possibilities (three to five funds), request prospectuses for each and devote an evening to comparing them.

A prospectus is usually not fun to read. The document contains a certain amount of jargon and some legal terms (despite recent rules by the Securities and Exchange Commission that encourage the use of plain English in the prospectus). But if you know what to look for, you're likely to find that the prospectus contains a wealth of information that can help you decide whether the fund is right for you.

Information contained in the standard prospectus includes

- The investment objective of the fund

- Investments the fund manager is allowed to make, even if they may not fit the stated objective

- The financial history of the fund for the past ten years, or, if the fund is younger than ten years, for the life of the fund

- The minimum amount of money required to invest

- The sales charges (loads) associated with investing, and when they are payable — at the front end (on purchasing shares), at the back end (when selling), or both

- The fund's operating expenses, including management charges, administrative expenses, and 12b-1 fees

- How to buy and sell shares and a description of shareholder services provided

Some funds have policies that allow the fund manager to invest in virtually anything — stocks, bonds, derivative securities, real estate, and what-have-you. I recommend that you avoid such funds, sticking instead with those that have clearly defined investment objectives.

The more prospectuses you read, the more familiar you can become with the terminology they use. By comparing prospectuses from several funds, you develop a sense of each fund's different personality. You probably find that one fund feels more comfortable to you than the others, which may be a sign that you've found a good prospect for your first investment experience.

CHAPTER 8

Buying a Mutual Fund

IN THIS CHAPTER

- Determining where, when, and how to buy mutual fund shares

- Buying through a broker or a fund supermarket

- Understanding the advantages of dollar cost averaging

With your research and decision-making accomplished, you are ready to buy! But there are choices to make concerning when and where to make your fund investments. Each mutual fund source has advantages and disadvantages that you'll want to weigh in making these choices. You should also consider using the investment techniques known as *dollar cost averaging,* which is a special fund buying method that can actually increase the rate of profit on your money.

Knowing Where to Buy

Investors use a wide range of channels to purchase mutual funds, but buying directly from the fund is the most popular, as you can see from the statistics in Table 8-1.

Table 8-1: Where Mutual Funds Are Bought by Percentage of Total Sales

Sales Outlet	Percentage of Total Sales
Fund company (direct)	40.3
Full-service broker	28.9
Fund company (indirect)	18.6

continued

Table 8-1: Where Mutual Funds Are Bought by Percentage of Total Sales (continued)

Sales Outlet	Percentage of Total Sales
Financial planner	12.7
Bank or credit union	9.7
Discount broker	6.0
Other (insurance brokers, certified public accountants, and other agents)	28.1

Buying directly from a fund company is the cheapest and most convenient way to buy for most investors. Just telephone the company of your choice and ask for an application. Complete the application form and send in your initial investment in the form of a check, and you're an investor — it's that simple.

(If you participate in a 401(k) plan or other employer-sponsored investment program, as I describe in Chapter 1, you may have the opportunity to buy shares from a fund company indirectly, through your company's investment plan. The paperwork and procedures are quite similar.)

Only a couple of the questions on the typical mutual fund application are likely to cause you any confusion. Expect to state how you want any capital gains and dividends handled (see Chapter 2 for more on the subject). You can have these profits paid to you in cash, or have them automatically reinvested in your account, buying more mutual fund shares.

I recommend that you reinvest profits from capital gains and dividends so that your investment portfolio can benefit from the power of compounding, as I explain in Chapter 1.

The mutual fund application may also ask whether you want

money each month from your checking account into the mutual fund of your choice.

If you're starting out with an investment program, I strongly recommend that you choose this option. After a few months, you won't even notice the money "missing" from your budget, but you can look forward to the satisfaction — excitement even — of the steady growth of your investment portfolio, as reflected in your monthly or quarterly statements.

Not all investors choose to buy mutual fund shares directly from fund companies. Some prefer to invest through full-service brokers, financial planners, or their bank or credit union (as noted in Table 8-1). Investing in this way has one significant advantage and one major disadvantage.

The advantage is the availability of investment advice and guidance. A good broker, planner, or banker should be willing to spend time analyzing your personal financial situation and be capable of offering unbiased, thoughtful suggestions concerning the best investment options for you. He or she should also have printed materials to share with you giving information about funds, investment strategies, economic forecasts, and other useful data. If you want this kind of help, consider consulting one of these financial professionals.

The disadvantage is the cost associated with this professional help. Full-service brokers, financial planners, and banks generally sell load funds rather than no-load funds.

As I explain in Chapter 6, load funds charge sales fees, often significant ones, whenever you buy shares. These fees can have a real impact on your investment profits. And, as I mention in Chapter 6, studies show that the investment performance of load funds is no better than that of no-load funds.

Therefore, the sales fees you pay buy the services of your broker, planner, or banker, but not an improvement in investment profits. It's up to you to decide whether the professional's advice is worth the expense.

If you invest through a broker, planner, or bank, you may also have to deal with the confusing phenomenon of *share classes,* which I explain later in this chapter.

Fund Supermarkets

A relatively new phenomenon in the mutual fund world are so-called *fund supermarkets.* These allow you to buy funds from several fund families for no or low transaction costs and to manage all your money in a single account. It's a convenient way to get access to literally thousands of mutual funds from a single source.

The fund supermarkets are managed by some of the leading *discount brokerage* firms — financial companies that specialize in no-frills investment buying and selling services for individual investors. Such firms as Charles Schwab, Muriel Siebert, Jack White, and National Discount Brokers are among those running fund supermarkets.

If you open an account with one of these firms, you'll be able to buy and sell shares from a wide range of fund families; switch from one fund to another with ease, even if the funds are in different families; and receive information about all your accounts in a single statement.

Deciding When to Buy

Be careful about buying shares in a mutual fund during the last quarter of the year (that is, during the months of October, November, and December). Most funds announce their last quarter of the year (that is, during the months of October, November, and December). Most funds announce their dividends, capital gains, and other such profits for the year during this quarter. The actual payment of these profits to shareholders (called the *distribution*) usually doesn't take place until January.

However, according to Internal Revenue Service rules, these profits are considered paid on December 31, and anyone who is a shareholder as of that date must pay taxes on them. Thus, you're probably better off waiting until after the January distribution to invest. You can receive the benefits of the profits, but you won't have to pay a tax bill on them because you were *not* a shareholder as of December 31.

Deciphering Differences in Share Classes

If you buy a mutual fund from a broker, financial planner, or banker rather than directly from the mutual fund company, you may run into a confusing variety of *share classes.* These different classes of shares have varying fee structures, and choosing among them can be tricky.

You can avoid this complication by sticking to a no-load fund and buying direct. (Chapter 6 tells you all about load and no-load funds.) But if buying a load fund from a broker, planner, or banker interests you, you may need to know the differences in class shares:

- **Class A shares:** These usually involve paying a sales charge (load) up front. The typical front-end load is in the neighborhood of 5.75%, but it may be higher or lower.

- **Class B shares:** You don't have a front-end sales charge on these shares, but you do have a 12b-1 fee (see Chapter 5), which is usually 1% a year. In addition, expect a years after buying, you may be charged 4%; between years three and four, 3%, and so on. Typically, after year six, you may have no charge.

■ **Class C shares:** These involve a so-called level load, which means they may charge a front-end charge of 1% plus a 1% annual 12b-1 fee.

Which class of shares offers the best deal? No single right answer exists. Although the high front-end load of the Class A shares sounds scary, paying the 5% once may be cheaper than paying 1% annually over (say) a 10-year investment period.

To further complicate matters, in many cases, a B share or C share automatically converts to Class A after a period of time. The quicker B shares convert to A, the better, because this conversion eliminates the annual 1% fee.

Unfortunately, share classes are not regulated and may vary from one fund company to another. Sometimes, only specific groups of investors are able to invest in special share classes.

For example, a certain share class may be designed for those who participate in 401(k) retirement plans. When buying a mutual fund through a broker, financial planner, or banker, be sure to ask about share classes and make certain you know what fees you will be charged.

If you want to avoid the confusing share classes, opt for a no-load fund. No-load funds have no front-end sales charges or other loads to figure out. (See Chapter 6 for more information on mutual fund fees and expenses.)

Dollar Cost Averaging

Dollar cost averaging is a technique whereby an investor puts a fixed amount of money into the same investment vehicle at regular intervals. For example, if Ian invests $500 a month into a mutual fund every month, he is dollar cost averaging.

Dollar cost averaging offers a number of benefits. For many investors, the habit of investing regularly is a difficult one to develop and maintain. Setting aside the same amount of money from each paycheck is a good way to develop this discipline.

Many mutual fund companies can arrange automatic deductions from your checking or savings account which make it even easier to invest regularly. You'll soon find that you hardly miss the money which is going to build a steadily increasing investment nest egg.

Dollar cost averaging also increases the rate of return on your investment dollar. Here's how it works. Suppose Ian invests his $500 a month into a mutual fund whose net asset value per share varies between $20 and $40. During months when the NAV is lower, Ian's $500 will enable him to buy more shares; when the NAV is higher, he'll buy fewer shares.

The beauty of dollar cost averaging is that, over time, by investing the same amount each month, Ian will buy more shares at a relatively lower price. Therefore, his average price per share will be lower, meaning that his investment profits will be greater.

See Table 8-2 for an illustration of how this works. Over the year shown, with the NAV of Ian's Fund F varying between $20 and $40 per share, the average NAV is $30.08 per share (calculated simply by adding the average monthly NAV — $20 in January, $24 in February, and so on — and then dividing the sum by 12). But Ian has been able to buy a total of more than 208 shares for $6,000. Thus, the average per-share price Ian has actually paid is just $28.83 — more than a dollar less than the average NAV for the period.

Dollar cost averaging always works this way: By buying more shares when the price goes down, you reduce your per-share purchase price and so stretch your investing dollar.

Table 8-2: Dollar Cost Averaging

$500 per month invested in Fund F, whose NAV varies between $20 and $40 per share. Shares purchased calculated by dividing $500 by the month's NAV.

Month	NAV	Shares Purchased
January	$20	25.00
February	24	20.83
March	28	17.86
April	22	22.73
May	26	19.23
June	34	14.71
July	40	12.50
August	37	13.51
September	33	15.15
October	30	16.67
November	32	15.63
December	35	14.29
Total shares purchased:	208.11	
Total purchase price:	$6,000.00 ($500/month x 12 months)	
Average purchase price:	$28.83	

Dollar cost averaging enables the investor to regard a decline in NAV not as a loss of value but rather an opportunity to buy more fund shares at a discount price. I strongly recommend it to all new investors — and to experienced ones who've never enjoyed its benefits.

CHAPTER 9

DEALING WITH TAXES

IN THIS CHAPTER

- Taxing dividends and capital gains

- Saving through tax-managed funds

- Cutting taxes by investing in tax-advantaged funds and municipal bond funds

- Saving toward retirement with tax-deferred IRAs, Roth IRAs, and 401(k)s

As a mutual fund investor, you may find great joy in seeing that your fund is providing substantial returns. But in most cases, you have to face a downside: taxes to be paid on the profits you enjoy. In this chapter, I explain how mutual fund profits are taxed and some of the strategies you can use to reduce the amount you must pay to Uncle Sam.

Tax Consequences of Mutual Fund Profits

As I cover in Chapter 2, you can profit in three ways when you own a mutual fund: through any increase in the net asset value (NAV) of the fund shares; through dividends; and through capital gains. Each of these kinds of profit has a potential impact on the taxes you have to pay.

For most investors, tax considerations are *not* worthy of top ranking on the list of concerns that may affect decisions about buying or selling a mutual fund. Most people are wise to buy and sell mutual funds based on their changing financial goals and their perceptions of the investment markets and the over-all economy rather than worrying too much about the relatively small tax consequences of their decisions.

However, if you're in a higher tax bracket (31% to 39.6%), you may want to take the tax implications of your mutual fund investment decisions more seriously. Here are the things you need to know.

At least annually, a mutual fund must distribute to investors the dividends and capital gains that the fund's portfolio has generated over the course of the year. As I explain in Chapter 2, dividends are a portion of the profits generated by a company and shared with those who own stock in the company, and capital gains represent the difference between the price at which you purchased a security and the higher price at which you sold it — the profits.

Bond funds usually distribute the income received from their investments in the form of a monthly dividend. Stock (equity) funds and balanced funds, which hold both stocks and bonds, may distribute dividends quarterly, annually, or semiannually.

Capital gains are distributed once a year. Around the end of the calendar year, the mutual fund company sends you a 1099-DIV (see Figure 9-1) form detailing the taxable distributions that you received during the year. You use this information when preparing your income tax return for submission by the following April 15.

Figure 9-1: A sample 1099-DIV Form.

9191 ☐ VOID ☐ CORRECTED

PAYER'S name, street address, city, state, ZIP code, and telephone no.	1 Ordinary dividends $ 2a Total capital gain distr. $	OMB No. 1545-0110 1999 Form 1099-DIV	Dividends and Distributions	
PAYER'S Federal identification number / RECIPIENT'S identification number	2b 28% rate gain $	2c Unrecap. sec. 1250 gain $	Copy A For Internal Revenue Service Center	
RECIPIENT'S name	2d Section 1202 gain $	3 Nontaxable distributions $	File with Form 1096.	
Street address (including apt. no.)	4 Federal income tax withheld $	5 Investment expenses $	For Privacy Act and Paperwork Reduction Act Notice and instructions for completing this form, see the	
City, state, and ZIP code	6 Foreign tax paid $	7 Foreign country or U.S. possession	1999 Instructions for Forms 1099, 1098, 5498, and W-2G.	
Account number (optional) / 2nd TIN Not. ☐	8 Cash liquidation distr. $	9 Noncash liquidation distr. $		

Form 1099-DIV Cat. No. 14415N Department of the Treasury - Internal Revenue Service

Dividends

Unless you invest your money in a tax-deferred retirement account (as explained later in this chapter), dividends you receive in the form of a distribution are generally treated as taxable income. Currently, the government taxes dividends at the ordinary federal income tax rate of 15% to 39.6%, depending on your overall taxable income.

You generally have a choice (selected when you open your mutual fund account) of receiving dividend distributions in the form of a payment by check or reinvesting them in the purchase of additional shares of the fund. Don't fall for the myth that if you reinvest the dividends you receive, the dividends are *not* taxable.

Unfortunately, that wishful thinking is not true. Although you never actually see the dividends in the form of cash, the dividends reinvested on your behalf during the year appear on your 1099-DIV form, and the IRS expects payment of all taxes due on these dividends.

If you want to avoid paying taxes on dividend income, you can opt to invest in a growth fund or a small cap fund. Such funds generally pay lower dividends than large cap funds or income funds, because they invest in small companies that use their profits to finance business expansion rather than paying dividends to investors. As a result, you're likely to receive lower dividends while enjoying greater profits in the form of net asset value growth.

However, the positive tax effect of lower dividends may be spoiled if the fund's rate of turnover is unusually high. If the fund manager buys and sells stocks frequently, the fund is likely to experience greater than average capital gains, on which the individual investor must also pay taxes.

So, if you choose a fund partly to avoid heavy tax payments, make sure to check its turnover rate before investing. (Chapter 6 gives more detail on how to analyze a fund's turnover rate.)

As I note later in this chapter, you can also delay or avoid some tax liabilities for dividend income by choosing a tax-exempt municipal bond fund or by putting your mutual fund investments in a tax-deferred account, such as an IRA or 401(k).

Capital gains

Capital gains — profits from an increase in the value of the securities held by the mutual fund — may be either *realized* or *unrealized.* Their tax status differs accordingly, with only realized profits being eligible for taxation. Here's how it works.

Capital gains are realized when the fund manager sells stocks (or, less commonly, bonds) at a price greater than their purchase price. When stocks held by the fund increase in price but are still held, the capital gains are unrealized.

Capital gains are taxed only when they are realized. For example, suppose Sharon owns shares of Fund M, whose net asset value increases by 10% during the course of a year due to a 10% increase of the value of the stocks owned by the fund. If the fund manager sold no securities during the year, the investor would receive no realized gains in the current year — therefore, no taxes due on capital gains.

However, suppose Sharon decides to sell her shares of Fund M. (Maybe she needs to cash in her investment in order to make a down payment on a new house.) When she does so, she is realizing (literally "making real") the profits earned by the fund due to the increase in the value of the stocks it owns. These profits are now capital gains on which Sharon is obligated to pay taxes.

Tip

If you plan to sell your mutual fund shares, consider the tax implications of your timing. If the value of your shares has grown significantly, so that you can expect a large tax payment, consider whether you want to accelerate the transaction (making the sale by December of the current year) or to delay it (pushing it back into next January), depending on which year your income may be greater.

Realizing your profits and paying taxes on them may be less painful during a year when your income is smaller and your tax rate is therefore lower.

Current tax law also distinguishes between *short-term* and *long-term capital gains.* Short-term capital gains are profits from sales of securities held by the fund for 18 months or less. The government taxes these gains at the same rate as ordinary income, just like dividends. In fact, you will actually find short-term capital gains listed in the "dividend income" box on your Form 1099-DIV because the tax rate is the same.

Long-term capital gains, on the other hand, are profits from the sale of securities held by the fund for longer than 18 months. These profits are taxed at a more favorable rate. If you are in the 15% tax bracket, the government taxes any long-term capital gains you enjoy taxed at just 10%; if you are in the 28% bracket or higher, your long-term capital gains are taxed at 20%.

As you can see by its design, federal tax law encourages investors — including fund managers — to hold on to securities for a longer time. Taxing long-term capital gains less heavily than short-term capital gains is another reason why a mutual fund with a lower turnover rate may be more beneficial for the investor than a fund that buys and sells stocks rapidly.

Tax-Managed Funds

Tax-managed funds are those in which tax effects are incorporated in the fund manager's decision-making process. The manager of such a fund is guided in her buying and selling decisions, in part, by considerations of how to avoid incurring excessive capital gains taxes in any given year.

For example, suppose that Jane Goodbucks is the manager of Fund T, a tax-managed fund. Jane may be contemplating selling the fund's shares of Microsoft, the giant software company, because she and her research staff expect the value of Microsoft stock to increase at a rate of just 10% a year during the next several years — a little lower than Jane would like. Jane is considering replacing her Microsoft stock with shares of Amazon.com, the online retailer, which she expects to grow at 11% a year.

If Jane ignores tax effects, she is likely to sell the Microsoft stock and buy Amazon.com. But because Fund T is a tax-managed fund, Jane first considers the cost her shareholders can expect to incur for capital gains. The taxes due will depend on the amount of the gains realized, which will depend, in turn, on how long Fund T held Microsoft and how far the stock increased during that time.

Based on these considerations, Jane may or may not decide to sell Microsoft. Due to the effect of taxes, trading Microsoft for Amazon.com may result in lower returns for investors, so holding the Microsoft shares may be the better choice.

You can find out whether a fund is tax-managed by reading the fund prospectus (learn more about that subject in Chapter 7). Unless the prospectus states otherwise, assume the fund is *not* tax-managed. If tax considerations are important to you, consider focusing your fund choices specifically on those that are managed with tax effects in mind.

Tax-advantaged mutual funds

Tax-advantaged mutual funds are funds whose investment holdings are designed to minimize the investor's tax liability. They may or may not be tax-managed, but their approach tends to be tax-efficient over time, resulting in overall lower tax payments by investors.

Index funds are the premier form of tax-advantaged investment. As I explain in Chapter 4, index funds feature a passive style of investing, in which the fund manager buys and sells stocks only as needed to ensure that the fund continues to mirror the index on which it's modeled.

Because the manager of an index fund doesn't do a lot of trading, relatively low amounts of capital gains are realized during any given year, minimizing the tax bite you must pay.

Perhaps the most tax-efficient fund type available today is an index fund that is specifically managed to minimize capital gains distributions. This involves certain accounting practices that the fund manager must be careful to follow, including identifying for the Internal Revenue Service the bought and sold *specific shares* of a given company.

By selling first all shares bought at a higher price and holding on to those bought at a lower price, a fund manager can reduce taxable distributions to investors significantly.

If you're interested in a tax-advantaged mutual fund, contact Charles Schwab and Vanguard. These two mutual fund companies are among those that offer tax-efficient index funds specifically designed to keep capital gains taxes as low as possible.

Municipal bond funds

A municipal bond fund is another kind of tax-advantaged mutual fund. As I detail in Chapter 5, a municipal bond fund invests in bonds issued by state, county, city, and other local government agencies. Most income from these bonds is exempt from federal income taxes (although you must report the income on your federal income tax return).

If you live in a state that levies a high state income tax, such as New York, California, or Massachusetts, you may want to consider a *single-state fund,* which invests in municipal bonds issued only in that state. Income from such a fund is exempt from state taxes as well as federal taxes, and may even be exempt from local taxes in a city (like New York) that levies a local income tax. Over 600 such single-state funds are currently available, covering some 30 states.

Despite the tax advantages of single-state funds, they're not for every investor. Some single-state portfolios are relatively risky. Because the fund manager is restricted to buying bonds issued in one state only, he may be forced to invest in some counties or government agencies whose credit is shaky. If the agency defaults on its obligations — that is, if it fails to make timely payment of the interest due on its bonds — the value of the portfolio may suffer significantly.

Study the prospectus of any municipal bond fund you are considering buying, and make sure you understand the degree of safety or risk involved with the bond investments held in the portfolio.

If safety is especially important to you, consider a municipal bond fund that invests only in *insured bonds.* These are bonds guaranteed by an independent agency that promises to make timely interest payments if the issuing agency runs into financial difficulties.

The prospectus for any fund you're considering states whether the portfolio includes insured bonds. The safety does come at a cost; generally speaking, an insured bond fund has a return that is 0.1% to 0.4% lower per year than an uninsured bond fund. You have to decide whether this lower return is a reasonable tradeoff for you.

Although interest and dividends from municipal bond funds are not taxable, capital gains (if any) generally are. Be careful to distinguish the different forms of income and treat them correctly on your tax return.

Tax-Deferred Retirement Accounts

If your primary investment goal is retirement, taxes need not be a major issue. Thanks to federal laws designed to encourage retirement savings, several special kinds of investment accounts are currently available that enable you to save on current taxes as you invest for retirement. Any mutual fund investment can enjoy major tax benefits if it is placed in one of these tax-deferred retirement accounts.

Every smart investor who is putting away money for a comfortable old age owes it to himself or herself to open such an account. As you can see in Table 9-1, your money grows much faster in a tax-deferred account than in an ordinary account.

Table 9-1:   Growth of a Taxable versus a Tax-Deferred Investment Account

Growth of a $2,000 annual investment with a 9% annual compounded growth rate, assuming a 28% federal income tax rate. Source: T. Rowe Price Associates Inc.

After Year	Taxable	Tax-Deferred
15	$51,400	$64,000
20	82,500	111,500
25	125,100	184,600
30	183,300	297,200

Here's a basic guide to the kinds of tax-deferred retirement accounts currently available under United States law.

Individual Retirement Accounts (IRAs)

Any American whose income is below a legally specified level can save up to $2,000 per year in an IRA account tax-free. This means that you pay no income taxes on the money you invest in your IRA, and the interest, dividends, and other income enjoyed by the money continues to be tax-free for as long as you let the investment grow. When you retire and begin withdrawing the IRA money, the funds are taxed as ordinary income at your applicable tax rate — which is likely to be lower than your current tax rate, because you no longer earn a salary.

Check current tax law to find out whether you're eligible for an IRA account. The answer will depend on your income and on whether you're covered by your employer's pension plan. If you're not covered by such a plan, you're fully eligible for the IRA tax deduction; if you are covered, the income limits kick in.

Any mutual fund company, brokerage firm, bank, or other financial company can help you set up an IRA account. You can then fund it with whatever investment you choose, including your choice of mutual fund.

When investing in an IRA or any other tax-deferred retirement plan, *don't* invest in a municipal bond fund or in any other fund type that specializes in low-tax or no-tax investing. Remember, such funds generally produce a lower rate of return than similar taxable funds, and because you are *not* paying any taxes on the income you enjoy from the fund, you have no reason to settle for that lower rate.

Roth IRAs

The Roth IRA is a new type of retirement account with significant advantages for most investors. Unlike a traditional IRA, the money you contribute to a Roth IRA is taxable at the time you invest it.

However, the income enjoyed by your Roth IRA account is not taxed, nor is the money in the account when you withdraw and spend it after retirement. This is a huge tax break, because your $2,000 annual contribution is likely to have grown into tens of thousands of dollars by the time you retire — all of which will be yours to use, tax-free.

Generally speaking, the only people for whom a traditional IRA is probably a better deal than the Roth IRA are those who are less than ten years away from retirement. For them, the immediate deductibility of this year's contribution may be worth more than the back-end deductibility of the Roth IRA.

Your broker, banker, or mutual fund company can help you with the calculations if you're unsure which type of account is better for you.

SEP-IRAs

This is a special type of IRA for people who run their own small businesses (the acronym SEP stands for "self-employed person"). If you're a freelancer, a temporary worker, or a self-employed professional of any kind, look into a SEP-IRA account. This account enables you to invest up to 15% of your annual earnings in a retirement account free of current taxes — a significant advantage over the ordinary IRA.

Another similar type of account is called the *Keogh plan.* The plan enables self-employed people to set aside even more tax-free income — usually up to 20% of your annual earnings — but the process involves a significant amount of paperwork, which may not sound particularly appealing to you.

401(k)s

Like an IRA, a 401(k) account enables you to save and invest for retirement with no current taxation either on the money you set aside or on the profits that accumulate over the years. You pay taxes on the money in your account only when you withdraw it after retirement.

The main difference is that your employer must sponsor your 401(k) account. Most for-profit companies today offer 401(k) plans; in fact, the 401(k) plan has become the most common substitute for the traditional company-paid pension plan, which fewer and fewer firms now provide.

As soon as you start any new job, ask about whether your employer offers a 401(k) plan and how you can begin to participate. Generally, this kind of plan is a wonderful deal for you. You can usually save any amount up to 10% or 15% of your salary, tax-free, with the money automatically deducted from your paycheck. (And,, this form of automatic saving is a great way to make regular investing a habit.)

Many employers match all or part of the employee contribution: For example, if you set aside 10% of your weekly paycheck for your 401(k) account, your company may kick in half that amount on top of your own contribution.

You can invest your 401(k) money in any investment vehicle offered by your employer. Most companies today make arrangements with large financial firms, including mutual fund companies, to provide an array of investment choices for their employees.

You're likely to have stock funds, bond funds, money market funds, and other options to choose from, and you can divide your contributions among two or more fund types if you want. You receive regular statements about the growth of your account, just as with any mutual fund or brokerage account.

If you leave your job, you will probably have the option of maintaining your 401(k) account, letting your money continue to grow tax-free until you retire. However, if you choose to receive the money in your account instead, you have to pay taxes and an IRS penalty on it — unless you roll your investment over into a rollover IRA, a new 401(k), or another type of tax-deferred account. Any fund company, broker, banker, or other financial professional can help you with the paperwork and other details.

A 403(b) is a similar type of account offered to employees of nonprofit organizations — schools, hospitals, and so on.

If you have the option of participating in a 401(k) or 403(b) plan at your place of work, sign up as soon as you can. For almost every investor, these plans are a great way to grow your money tax-free, usually with help from your employer. Your 401(k) account can become the backbone of your savings plan for a happy and secure retirement.

CHAPTER 10

MUTUAL FUND SERVICES

- Looking into mutual fund account statements

- Seeking information and performing transactions via phone and online

- Making use of check-writing, automatic investment and reinvestment, and other services

When selecting a mutual fund for your investment dollars, you need to evaluate the services that the fund company offers. Some questions to ask include

- Will I have 24-hour phone access to my account?

- Can I conduct transactions via the Internet?

- How much information will be included in my account statements?

You may be influenced to choose one fund company over another because it offers more useful services for shareholders. In this chapter, you learn about some of the services available and how to make the most of the benefits they offer.

Understanding Basic Services

The basic services that you can expect from any mutual fund company include the following:

- Regular written reports on the performance of your investments

- 24-hour, toll-free customer service

- The ability to exchange money between funds in the same family with relative ease and at little or no cost

- The ability to make additional investments easily and quickly

- The choice between having dividends and capital gains paid directly to you or reinvested in additional mutual fund shares

- Check-writing capabilities

- Professional advisory services

Beyond these basics, however, more and more mutual fund families are offering services that go above and beyond the call of duty. For some investors, the variety and quality of shareholder services provided is an important factor in choosing a fund or fund family in which to invest.

It's also important to keep in mind that the *quality* of basic services varies from one fund company to another. For example, account statements highlight the differences among various companies' approaches.

Account statements

Although every mutual fund provides shareholders with periodic reports on their investments, the quality, understandability, and comprehensiveness of these reports vary widely.

Most mutual fund families provide quarterly statements that let you know what your current investment balance is, how many shares you own in each fund you've invested in, and your current *asset allocation* (that is, what percentage of your money is invested in which types of funds). In addition, the statement lists the transactions on your account since the last statement — new share purchases and redemptions; switching of money from one fund to another; dividend reinvestments; capital gain distributions, and so on.

If you have more than one mutual fund investment with the same family, you typically receive a combined statement showing all of your holdings rather than a separate statement for each fund. You also get a year-end statement for tax purposes, which shows balances and account activity for the entire year.

The account statements provided by most mutual fund companies provide the basics; only a few offer the luxuries. Dalbar, Inc., an independent financial research company located in Boston, has developed quality rankings for account statements from various mutual fund companies. According to Dalbar, the top account statements, in ranking order, come from the following fund companies:

- The WM group of funds
- Kemper Funds
- Montgomery Funds
- The Dreyfus family of funds
- The MFS family of funds

Why did Dalbar rank the WM Funds at the top of its list? Beyond the basics, WM provides investors with such data as their beginning and ending account balance for the statement period, the total account value, and the total return percentage per fund.

For investors who participate in the company's asset allocation advisory services program, WM Funds reports the total return on investors' asset allocation portfolios — a collection of investments in various categories that shifts over time in response to changes in market and economic conditions.

Eventually, WM hopes to provide investors with personalized returns under this program, showing total return on a shareholder's own asset allocation account. Like most good fund companies, WM is constantly looking for ways to apply new information technology to communicate data to investors more quickly and usefully.

Dalbar says that most fund investors are dissatisfied with their account statements for several basic reasons:

- The statement provides too much information. Although investors need complete data on their accounts, a fine line exists between comprehensiveness and overkill. When too much information appears on the account statement, an investor may feel overwhelmed. Fund companies are beginning to refine and improve their presentation of information by selectively eliminating less-useful data and by making the data they retain easier to read through intelligent design and use of graphics. For example, many funds now show an investor's current asset allocation percentages using a pie chart rather than simply listing a set of numbers.

- The report requires investors to translate tricky mathematical terminology. For example, some fund companies provide statistics like "average cost per share" (a number that may be useful when calculating the taxes due on mutual fund shares you've sold), but they don't describe how it was derived. This lack of information forces you to figure it out yourself. The best account statements explain the source and meaning of every number presented.

- The statement overestimates the investor's knowledge. Fund companies often use language that the typical investor doesn't understand. The best account statements include a brief glossary with definitions of technical terms.

When you invest in a new fund, study the first account statement carefully. Make sure that you understand every piece of data it includes. If you don't, call the fund company's information line and ask the representative to walk you through the statement, number by number.

Jot down notes as you go. And don't be afraid to ask "silly questions"! Having read this book, you know *more* than the average investor, so your questions are probably not foolish at all. After all, your money is at stake here — you deserve to know exactly what it's doing.

24-hour phone lines

You don't need to wait for a quarterly statement to get answers about your mutual fund account. Today, most fund families make information about your account as near as your telephone.

Some major fund families offer 24-hour phone lines staffed by real human beings — a welcome convenience for the millions of investors who find themselves living such busy lives that the only time they have to check their investments may be at 11:00 on a Wednesday night or 8:30 Sunday morning.

Other fund families have phone lines with live representatives only during business hours; however, they usually provide a 24-hour automated response phone system that gives you access to your account balance and the current NAV of your shares and enables you to make exchanges between funds simply by using your telephone keypad. Your own coded *personal identification number* (PIN) protects your privacy, so only you can access the account.

Tip

On occasion, you may need to open a mutual fund account in a hurry. For example, you may want to make a qualifying IRA deposit on April 15 so that you meet the annual deadline for saving on your taxes (see Chapter 9 for more on tax considerations).

Many mutual fund companies are willing to let you open an account and make a deposit by phone, even without a completed application on file, provided you submit the application soon thereafter. Call the fund of your choice, explain the situation, and provide the information the company requests, including the number of your bank account where the necessary investment money is on deposit. Then have your bank wire the money to the fund.

Online information and transactions

With the advent of the Internet, most mutual fund companies now offer the same information online that you receive in your printed account statements. In addition, you can access many other types of data and services online, which relieves much of the time and effort involved in doing research via multiple phone calls, letters, or office visits.

For example, at the Vanguard Web site (www.vanguard.com), you can find such information as

- Historical data on how particular funds have performed
- The largest stock or bond holdings of particular funds
- Specific data about your accounts

Most of the things you do over the phone, you can also do online. For example, you can make investment exchanges between funds, request redemptions, and buy shares.

You can also download application forms and fund prospectuses, plus you can locate other literature on Web sites. Typically, you can access marketing brochures, articles on retirement investing, and speeches by officials at the fund company.

With each passing month, fund families are offering more and more interesting online perks. You can look forward to finding retirement calculators, reports on the economy, glossaries of investment terms, mini-courses on investment fundamentals, and other services.

Vanguard, for example, offers WebTurboTax tax-return software free to its online shareholders. Many fund Web sites feature message boards and chat rooms where you can share information and questions with other investors or with the company guru who can respond to your inquiries.

The Resource Center at the back of this book lists some of the more useful mutual fund Web sites, including those sponsored by fund companies and those established by independent companies or organizations.

Automatic investment and reinvestment plans

Most fund families make it easy to set up an automatic investment plan, which is an excellent way for you to develop a consistent practice of saving. When you opt for automatic contributions to an investment account, you can also take advantage of the benefits of dollar cost averaging (refer to Chapter 8).

Ask your fund company for information about how to establish an automatic investment plan. You determine the amount that you want to designate — $100, $300, $1,000 — and the sum automatically comes out of your bank account each month and is invested in the fund of your choice. Plan to complete an application form and send in a (voided) check from your bank account.

You can also have the dividends and capital gains income from your funds automatically reinvested, buying you additional shares. I strongly recommend reinvesting, because it allows you to enjoy the benefits of compounding, as I explain in Chapter 1.

Most fund families will allow you to have your dividend and capital gains income reinvested in a *different* fund, which can be an easy way of diversifying your portfolio.

Suppose Jacob has $5,000 invested in an index fund — a conservative, low-cost form of stock investment. He can arrange to have the dividends and capital gains from this fund invested in the fund family's Aggressive Growth fund. As this amount gradually builds up, the growing investment gives Jacob the opportunity to participate in the profit potential of a more risky and volatile but often lucrative sector of the stock market — without taking any money out of his lower-risk index fund investment.

Check-writing

If you own shares in a bond fund, such as a money market fund, you probably have the option of writing checks against the money in your account on special checks from the fund company. (Check-writing is normally *not* an option with a stock fund.)

Most funds establish a minimum amount for the checks you write (typically $500), and you may have a small per-check charge. Writing a check can be a convenient way of redeeming shares.

When you write a check against a mutual fund, whether to raise some cash or to pay a bill, you are redeeming shares of your investment. Thus, you may be realizing capital gains or other profits, which subjects you to a tax liability at the end of the year. Don't forget this potential for taxable profit when the time comes to perform your tax calculations.

Retirement-related services

Many fund firms offer retirement planning services. You may be able to consult a staff member who is familiar with retirement planning issues by telephone, or you may have access to retirement-planning brochures, worksheets, and other literature through the mail or online.

Typically, the retirement topics covered include the following:

- How to calculate the amount of money you can expect to require for a comfortable and secure retirement

- How much you need to save and invest each month in order to reach your retirement goals

- How your asset allocation should change over time as your investment time horizon and risk tolerance change

- The pros and cons of various kinds of tax-advantaged retirement accounts: IRAs, Roth IRAs, 401(k)s, Keogh plans, and so on

- Options for taking distributions from your retirement account

Social Security plays a role in retirement planning for most Americans. Despite concerns over the long-term viability of the government funding for Social Security, most people can expect to derive at least part of their retirement income from this source.

Your Social Security income will be based largely on how much money you've earned (and paid Social Security taxes on) throughout your life. To determine how much you're probably going to receive from the government after retirement, request Form SSA-7004, the Personal Earnings and Benefit Estimate Statement, from the Social Security Administration, by calling toll-free 1-800-772-1213 or by logging onto their Web site at www.ssa.gov.

When you receive the statement (in four to six weeks), you can develop some perspective on your expected monthly Social Security payments — and how much more retirement income you'll need to provide through your own savings and investments.

Advisory services

Most mutual fund investors are self-directed: They educate themselves through books like this one, personal finance magazines and TV programs, and brochures and prospectuses offered by the fund companies. Then they make their fund selections and monitor the growth of their investments in order to make sure that they perform as expected. One reason for the popularity of mutual funds is that they lend themselves to just this kind of do-it-yourself investing.

However, the bigger fund companies do offer free, personalized advisory services to their higher-dollar clients — especially those with assets of $500,000 or more.

Most people who give advice are Certified Financial Planners (look for the CFP designation after their names). Their expertise covers asset allocation approaches, investment strategies, and economic and business trends, and they're qualified to give specific recommendations on funds to consider. They may also talk about the tax implications of your investment.

If you are not (yet) a part of this investment stratosphere, you may be able to gain some of the same advice from a broker, accountant, insurance agent, or other professional.

Be sure you understand exactly how your advisor derives his compensation. An advisor who receives a fee directly from you for his services — either in the form of a straight payment or as a percentage of the assets you invest — is likely to give relatively unbiased advice (how knowledgeable or helpful this guidance proves to be is another matter).

On the other hand, advisors who receive all or part of their payments in the form of sales commissions may recommend that you buy the investment products from which they stand to benefit personally. A stockbroker may urge you to invest in stocks; an insurance agent may direct you toward insurance company products such as annuities. Before you buy into any sales pitch, carefully consider the source and what he or she has to gain from your investment.

CLIFFSNOTES REVIEW

Use this CliffsNotes Review to practice what you've learned in this book and to build your confidence as you begin your adventures in mutual funds investing. After you work through the review questions, the problem-solving exercises, and the thought-provoking practice projects, you'll be well on your way to achieving your goal of becoming a savvy mutual funds investor!

Q&A

1. Owning a mutual fund provides diversification for your investment funds because a mutual fund

    a. Is guaranteed by an agency of the federal government

    b. Owns many different stocks or bonds

    c. Is managed by a highly-educated money manager

2. When the price of stocks owned by a mutual fund increases, the investors in the fund benefit from

    a. An increase is the fund's net asset value

    b. The payment of dividends

    c. Savings on income taxes

3. Generally, the most conservative and least risky of the following three fund types is the

    a. Emerging market equity fund

    b. High-yield bond fund

    c. Money market fund

4. International equity funds are more risky than U.S.-only equity funds partly because of

    a. High rates of U.S. taxation on foreign investments

    b. The danger of changes in currency exchange rates

    c. The low dividends paid by foreign companies

5. A municipal bond fund is an appropriate investment choice for someone most concerned with

a. Reducing his or her tax payments

b. Having immediate access to his or her money

c. Rapid growth in the value of his or her investment

6. The main advantage of buying funds through a mutual fund supermarket is the availability of

a. Thousands of funds from a single source

b. Only the highest-rated funds in each fund category

c. Advice from a knowledgeable broker

7. Generally, you should consider buying shares of a closed-end mutual fund only when they are priced _____.

8. Regular dividends are most likely to be paid by

a. A young, quickly growing company

b. An old, established, and successful company

c. A company that is struggling to survive financially

9. The easiest way to determine the annual cost of investing in a particular fund is to look in the prospectus for the fund's

_____.

10. A balanced fund is one that invests in both

a. U.S. and foreign companies

b. Corporate and government bonds

c. Stocks and bonds

Answers: (1) b. (2) a. (3) c. (4) b. (5) a. (6) a. (7) At a discount to the net asset value (NAV). (8) b. (9) Expense ratio. (10). c.

Scenarios

1. You are 30 years old, and you are saving for retirement by invest-ing in a mid cap growth fund. One day you receive a quarterly statement from the fund showing that, during the past three months, the value of the investments in the fund has fallen by 10%. You should _____ _____.

2. Based on your reading and on personal business experience, you've become convinced that the health care industry is likely to experience major growth in sales and profits in the next 20 years. To enjoy the benefits of this growth through mutual fund investments, you should consider investing in _____.

3. You live in a city and state with high local and state income tax rates. To save the most on your federal, state, and local taxes, you should invest in _____.

Answers: (1) Stay invested; your investment time frame is a long one, which means that the fund has plenty of time to recover its value and resume steady growth. (2) A sector fund that specializes in the health care industry. (3) A triple tax-exempt municipal bond fund.

Consider This

■ Did you know that most mutual fund families can make it easy for you to invest a fixed amount every month through an auto-matic deduction from your checking account? It's a great way to make your savings grow painlessly with no need for self-discipline on your part. See Chapter 8 for more information about buying funds directly from fund management compa-nies.

■ Did you know that savings invested in an IRA, 401(k), or other type of tax-deferred account grow faster than in an ordinary investment account? Almost everyone is eligible to participate in one or more of these special plans. See Chapter 9 for more information on how to save on taxes as your retirement savings grow.

■ Did you know that index funds, which invest in all the stocks that are part of a particular stock market index, regularly outperform other types of mutual funds, while running up lower management fees? Growing numbers of investors are making index funds their favorite way to invest. See Chapter 4 for more information on index funds and how they work.

Practice Projects

1. Read the coverage of mutual funds in a recent issue of a financial magazine. Find the names and phone numbers of three mutual funds that interest you and request a copy of the prospectus for each (as explained in Chapter 7). Read the prospectuses and decide whether one of these funds might make a sound investment for you.

2. Visit your local library and ask to see reports from three of the following — Morningstar, Value Line, Lipper Analytical, and Wiesenberger — on any mutual fund in which you're interested. Compare the information presented in the three reports. Which do you find most understandable? Most interesting? Most helpful? See Chapter 7 for more information on using these reports.

3. List your three most important short-term financial goals and your three most important long-term financial goals (as I explain in Chapter 1). For each goal, estimate the amount of money you'll need to reach the goal and the number of months or years it will take to reach the goal. Then decide how much money you can set aside each month to invest in mutual funds in pursuit of these goals.

CLIFFSNOTES RESOURCE CENTER

The learning has just begun! CliffsNotes Resource Center shares information on outstanding print and online sources of additional information about mutual funds. The organizations, publications, and other sources listed here are popular, well-respected, authoritative voices in the financial industry, and I believe you can gain valuable insight from checking out what they have to offer. Look for these terrific resources at your favorite bookstore and on the Internet. When you're online make your first stop www.cliffnotes.com, where you'll find more incredibly useful information on mutual funds.

Books

This CliffsNotes book is one of many great books on mutual funds and investment topics published by IDG Books Worldwide, Inc. So if you want some great next-step books, check out these other publications.

CliffsNotes Investing for the First Time, by Tracey Longo, introduces you to commonly available investment options and invites you to create a plan with your newfound knowledge of investing. IDG Books — $8.99.

Investing For Dummies, by Eric Tyson, is the perfect book for people looking to develop an investment strategy. IDG Books — $19.99.

Investing Online For Dummies, 2nd Edition, by Kathleen Sindell, is an ideal guide to a vast array of Internet investment tools, links, and resources. IDG Books — $24.99.

Mutual Funds For Dummies, 2nd Edition, by Eric Tyson, gives you expert advice on making the most of your investment portfolio. IDG Books — $19.99.

Personal Finance For Dummies, 2nd Edition, by Eric Tyson, is a rich money-management resource for anyone who wants to enjoy the rewards of smart money management. IDG Books — $19.99.

How Mutual Funds Work, 2nd Edition, by Albert J. Fredman and Russ Wiles, is an authoritative guide to the technical aspects of fund investing. Filled with detail, this is a useful reference tool or the next step for a reader eager to learn much more about the world of mutual funds. New York Institute of Finance — $18.95.

But Which Mutual Funds? by Steven T. Goldberg, is a reader-friendly guide to devising your own investment plan and finding funds to fit it. Many of today's best funds in various fund categories are described and explained in easy-to-understand language. Kiplinger — $24.95.

Bogle on Mutual Funds, by John C. Bogle, is a guide to mutual fund investment strategies by the founder and chairman of the Vanguard family of funds. A particularly useful feature of the book is a chapter containing model fund portfolios for investors in five different financial and life situations. Irwin — $14.95.

A Commonsense Guide to Mutual Funds, by Mary Rowland, is built mainly around 70 two- to three-page explanations of key "Dos and Don'ts" for mutual fund investors, offering solid basic advice for smarter investing. Bloomberg Press — $15.95.

It's easy to find books published by IDG Books Worldwide, Inc. and other publishers. You can find them in your favorite bookstores (on the Internet and at stores near you). We also have three Web sites that you can use to read about all the books we publish:

- www.cliffnotes.com
- www.dummies.com
- www.idgbooks.com

Internet

Check out these Web sites for more information on mutual funds and other investment topics:

American Association of Individual Investors (AAII) at www.aaii.org is a nonprofit nationwide educational organization that publishes books and periodicals and sponsors seminars on investment strategies for individual investors.

Bloomberg.com at www.bloomberg.com is a leading source of current business, financial, and economic news.

The Investment Company Institute at www.ici.org is the official membership organization for the mutual fund industry — a source of data, statistics, and information on funds.

The Mutual Fund Education Alliance at www.mfea.com provides handy information collected from many mutual fund companies, along with educational articles on investing, lists of top funds in specific categories, and so on.

Quicken.com at www.quicken.com/investments features a variety of investment information from the makers of Quicken financial software, including a set of useful tools for performing investment calculations.

The No-Load Fund Investor at www.sheldonjacobs.com is a site with a large amount of useful data, including historical performance information on over 2,400 no-load funds.

Next time you're on the Internet, don't forget to drop by www.cliffsnotes.com. We created an online Resource Center that you can use today, tomorrow, and beyond.

Magazines & Newspapers

Most financial magazines and newspapers provide regular coverage of mutual funds. The following publications generally are considered the most authoritative and reliable.

Barron's is a weekly newspaper focusing on current investment trends, statistics, and strategies. In addition to interviews and forums with leading investment experts, it features very comprehensive tables tracking the performance of mutual funds, individual stocks and bonds, and most other popular investment vehicles (www.barrons.com). $3.00/issue.

Business Week is a weekly magazine covering general business news. It includes a weekly "Personal Investing" section that contains tips and ideas on mutual funds as well as other forms of investing, and special issues periodically track trends and performance statistics for the entire universe of mutual funds (www.businessweek.com). $3.95/issue.

Forbes is a biweekly magazine covering general business news, with special strength at analyzing the performance and prospects of individual companies and industry sectors. *Forbes* periodically devotes a special issue to mutual fund trends and performance (www.forbes.com). $4.95/issue.

Fortune is a weekly magazine covering general business news, especially personalities, management ideas, and industry trends. Special issues periodically focus on mutual fund trends and performance (www.pathfinder.com). $4.95/issue.

Kiplinger's Personal Finance Magazine is a monthly magazine that covers a wide range of personal money issues, including investing (especially in mutual funds), budgeting and saving, insurance, retirement, taxes, and consumer tips (www.kiplinger.com). $2.95/issue.

Money is a monthly magazine that covers all aspects of personal finance, from investing and saving to retirement planning, smart strategies for shopping and spending, and reducing your taxes. Mutual funds are covered extensively. (www.money.com). $3.95/issue.

Mutual Funds Magazine is a monthly magazine focusing exclusively on mutual fund investing. It includes profiles and interviews with fund managers, news about management changes and other developments at leading funds, and stories about how to use mutual funds as part of your overall personal finance strategy (www.mfmag.com). $2.95/issue.

Smart Money is a monthly magazine that focuses on personal investing. Founded in part by Fidelity, one of the major mutualfund families, it features the insights of Peter Lynch, perhaps the most famous mutual fund investment gurus in the world (www.smartmoney.com). $3.50/issue.

Worth is a monthly magazine that covers personal investing and other financial topics, including mutual funds. In tone and content, *Worth* is one of the most sophisticated periodicals in the field, probably most appropriate for the experienced or relatively affluent investor (www.worth.com). $3.00/issue.

You can find these publications at your neighborhood book-store. Visit the Web sites (or your local library) for an overview of the style and contents of each periodical.

Send Us Your Favorite Tips

In your quest for learning, have you ever experienced that sublime moment when you figure out a trick that saves time or trouble? Perhaps you realized you were taking ten steps to accomplish something that could have taken two. Or you've found a little-known workaround that gets great results. If you've discovered a useful tip that helped you make decisions about mutual funds more effectively, and you'd like to share it, CliffsNotes would love to hear from you. Go to our Web site at www.cliffsnotes.com and click the Talk to Us button. If we select your tip, we may publish it as part of CliffsNotes Daily, our exciting free e-mail newsletter. To find out more, or to subscribe to a newsletter, go to www.cliffnotes.com on the Web.

INDEX

SYMBOLS & NUMBERS

1099–DIV form, 35, 84
12b-1 fees. *See also* fees
401(k) retirement accounts, 12, 94
  share class considerations, 80
403(b) retirement accounts, 95

A

account statements, 97–100
active investing, 40
administrative costs, 61. *See also* fees
advantages of mutual funds
  diversification, 26
  liquidity, 30
  low entry cost, 28
  shareholder services, 30
aggressive growth funds, 44
annual operating expenses , 59
automatic investment plans, 76, 102

B

balanced funds, 54
bear markets, 32
"beating the indexes", 40
blue chip stocks, 42
bond funds, 64. *See also* balanced funds
  corporate, 53
  expense ratio, 62
  fees
    12b-1 fees, 63
    administrative costs, 61
    annual operating expenses, 59
    cost of turnover, 64
    expense ratio, 62
    load funds, 56
    management fees, 60
    no load funds, 58
    redemption fees, 57
  financial goals, matching with, 66
  insured bond funds, 90
  junk bonds, 54
  maturity dates, lack of, 36
  money market funds, 51
  municipal bond funds, 52, 90
    tax advantages, 52, 89
  risk, 50
  safety ratings
    Moody's, 53
    Standard & Poor's, 53

bonds
  defined, 17
bull markets, 32
buying funds
  from fund companies, 75
  full-service broker advantages, 77
  fund supermarkets, 78
  share class considerations, 79
  when to buy, tax considerations of, 78

C

capital gains, 22, 34
  long-term, 87
  realized/unrealized, 86
  short-term, 87
  tax consequences, 86
cash equivalent, 51
cashing in funds
  liquidity issues, 30
  price uncertainty, 35
  redemption fees, 57
Certified Financial Planners, 105
check writing on funds, 103
closed-end funds, 23–25
commissions, 57. *See* fees
compounding, 13–14
corporate bond funds, 53
cost of turnover, 64. *See also* fees
costs of mutual funds, 56. *See* fees
credit card debt, 12
currency risk of international funds, 46,
custodial fees, 61. *See also* fees

D

daily return, 20
derivative instruments, 45
disadvantages of mutual funds
  bond fund maturity dates missing, 36
  fund management risk, 31
  lack of insurance, 33
  market-related risk, 32
  tax inefficiency, 34
  uncertain redemption price, 35
discount brokers, 78
distribution (12b-1) fees, 63
diversification, 9, 27
dividends
  defined, 17
  distribution, 22, 78
  tax consequences, 85
dollar cost averaging, 75, 80–82
Dow Jones Industrial Average, 39

COMING SOON FROM CLIFFSNOTES

Online Shopping

HTML

Choosing a PC

Beginning Programming

Careers

Windows 98 Home Networking

eBay Online Auctions

PC Upgrade and Repair

Business

Microsoft Word 2000

Microsoft PowerPoint 2000

Finance

Microsoft Outlook 2000

Digital Photography

Palm Computing

Investing

Windows 2000

Online Research

IDG BOOKS WORLDWIDE

COMING SOON FROM CLIFFSNOTES
Buying and Selling on eBay

Have you ever experienced the thrill of finding an incredible bargain at a specialty store or been amazed at what people are willing to pay for things that you might toss in the garbage? If so, then you'll want to learn about eBay — the hottest auction site on the Internet. And CliffsNotes *Buying and Selling on eBay* is the shortest distance to eBay proficiency. You'll learn how to:

■ Find what you're looking for, from antique toys to classic cars

■ Watch the auctions strategically and place bids at the right time

■ Sell items online at the eBay site

■ Make the items you sell attractive to prospective bidders

■ Protect yourself from fraud

Here's an example of how the step-by-step CliffsNotes learning process simplifies placing a bid at eBay:

1. Scroll to the Web page form that is located at the bottom of the page on which the auction item itself is presented.

2. Enter your registered eBay username and password and enter the amount you want to bid. A Web page appears that lets you review your bid before you actually submit it to eBay. After you're satisfied with your bid, click the Place Bid button.

3. Click the Back button on your browser until you return to the auction listing page. Then choose View⇨Reload (Netscape Navigator) or View⇨Refresh (Microsoft Internet Explorer) to reload the Web page information. Your new high bid appears on the Web page, and your name appears as the high bidder.